T0355184

A Wild West of the Mind

A Wild West
of the Mind

GEORGE SHER

OXFORD
UNIVERSITY PRESS

OXFORD
UNIVERSITY PRESS

Oxford University Press is a department of the University of Oxford. It furthers
the University's objective of excellence in research, scholarship, and education
by publishing worldwide. Oxford is a registered trade mark of Oxford University
Press in the UK and certain other countries.

Published in the United States of America by Oxford University Press
198 Madison Avenue, New York, NY 10016, United States of America.

© Oxford University Press 2021

Library of Congress Cataloging-in-Publication Data
Names: Sher, George, author.
Title: A Wild West of the Mind / George Sher.
Description: New York, NY, United States of America :
Oxford University Press, 2021. | Includes bibliographical references and index.
Identifiers: LCCN 2020053787 (print) | LCCN 2020053788 (ebook) |
ISBN 9780197564677 (hb) | ISBN 9780197564691 (epub) |
ISBN 9780197564707 | ISBN 9780197564684
Subjects: LCSH: Thought and thinking—Moral and ethical aspects.
Classification: LCC BJ45.5 .S54 2021 (print) | LCC BJ45.5 (ebook) |
DDC 153.4/2—dc23
LC record available at https://lccn.loc.gov/2020053787
LC ebook record available at https://lccn.loc.gov/2020053788

DOI: 10.1093/oso/9780197564677.001.0001

1 3 5 7 9 8 6 4 2
Printed by Integrated Books International, United States of America

Contents

Preface and Acknowledgments

There are many ways to think of minds—as sets of states with interlocking functional roles, for example, or as coronas of sensation hovering over extremely complicated machines—but in my capacity as the lone inhabitant of one specific mind in which I take a particular interest, the image that means the most to me is that of a vast, unbounded, unregulated space. That's the image that my title's wild west metaphor captures, and it has shaped the writing of this book by allowing me to bring together a number of attitudes that I hold dear.

Perhaps the most important of these is my sheer delight in the variety and instinctive candor of thought—in its tendency to follow its nose, like a snuffling dog, into any pungent crevice of interest or truth. A second such attitude is my conviction that those in the philosophy business tend greatly to overmoralize—to depart from common sense by insisting that even the most ordinary of decisions and conflicts are fraught with deep moral meaning. Yet a third is my dismay at the broader culture's gathering hostility toward an ever-widening range of attitudes, emotions, and beliefs that don't fit the cultural narrative du jour. The book's title, when it popped up in a morning conversation with my like-minded wife, served immediately to highlight both the connections among these attitudes and the importance of exploring them in print. Galvanized, I went straight to work, first on a freestanding paper and then on a book to fill in the assumptions and arguments that the paper necessarily left unexplored.

Writing the book has been a labor of love. Addressing the prototype paper's unanswered questions was like blowing up an easily inflated balloon, one of the long narrow ones that are easily twisted into segmented dachshunds. At each stage, the writing drew urgency from conviction. Once, before presenting one of the book's chapters in a talk, I heard myself saying, "I always believe what I write, but this time I mean it." I still don't know quite what I meant when I said that, but I do know that whatever it was, I meant it.

The paper from which the book developed, also entitled "A Wild West of the Mind," first appeared in the *Australasian Journal of Philosophy* 97, no. 3 (2019): 483–96. I thank the publisher for permission to reprint some material from it here. I also want to thank the many friends and audience members who have provided valuable feedback on the project. I presented material from the book at the University of Warwick, the University of Arizona, the University of St. Thomas in Houston, the Rocky Mountain Ethics Congress in Boulder, Colorado, and the Second Workshop on Humanistic Ethics at Rice University, and I was privileged to attend a one-day workshop on the full manuscript at the Free University of Amsterdam. On each occasion, I received illuminating comments from more people than I can now remember, so I'll simply offer a collective "thank you" to all who contributed to those interesting discussions.

Thanks, too, to those who generously commented on the project in its various stages of development: Richard Arneson, Gwen Bradford, Anthony Carreras, Justin Coates, Thomas Hurka, Michael McKenna, Daniel Pallies, Philip Robichaud, Steven Wall, Jan-Willem Weiland, and two anonymous referees for the *Australasian Journal*. I owe a special debt to my colleague Vida Yao, who read the whole manuscript and had perceptive and illuminating things to say about each part of it. I couldn't wish for a better philosophical interlocutor.

My greatest debt is to my wife, Emily Fox Gordon, a marvelous writer who has supported and encouraged this project from the beginning and who, as it happened, was herself mining a related seam of ideas while I was writing the book. (Two of the essays she wrote during that period are cited in Chapter 6.) Our conversations about these subjects were the best kind of collaboration, with lots of amplifying, correcting, filling in, and egging on in both directions. It was a wonderful experience, and the book is much the better for it.

1

Nasty as I Wanna Be

A ramble through someone else's mind would not be a pleasant experience. Even if you didn't stumble across any fond memories of
snuff movies, and even if you encountered no pockets of lust for
eight-year-olds or lurid fantasies of torture, domination, or rape,
you could hardly avoid the many rank pools of resentment, jealousy, and schadenfreude. You'd also be likely to find many hostile attitudes toward nominal friends, negative and stereotyped
judgments of groups, and florid growths of contempt. There
would, of course, also be much that was pleasing: genuine affection for some, perhaps a judicious appreciation of merit in others,
and—one might hope—a generalized sense of goodwill and commitment to sound principles. Still, much of what you found would
be ugly and would invite justified moral condemnation if it were
externalized. Are we similarly entitled to condemn what is inside
when it is *not* externalized?

According to many, the answer is a resounding "yes." We are all
familiar with moral condemnation that is directed at purely private events—at forbidden thoughts and fantasies, inappropriate
emotions, beliefs that are unsupported (or, sometimes, supported!)
by evidence, and wayward attitudes, like the lust that once resided
in Jimmy Carter's heart. It seems to me, though, that all this
finger-wagging is badly mistaken and that the realm of the purely
mental is best regarded as a morality-free zone. Within that realm,
no thoughts or attitudes are either forbidden or required. In the
chapters that follow, I will argue that unlike actions in the world,
which morality is properly said to constrain, each person's subjectivity is a limitless, lawless wild west in which absolutely everything
is permitted.

A Wild West of the Mind. George Sher, Oxford University Press (2021). © Oxford University Press.
DOI: 10.1093/oso/9780197564677.003.0001

I

By "everything" I mean everything, and it will be helpful to begin with a few examples. Although I cannot prove it, I am convinced that every living human being is often bloody-minded and even more often dirty-minded and that there is no day in anyone's life in which he does not have thoughts that he would not dream of expressing. Although there are of course limits of both decorum and self-protection to how far one can go by way of illustration—everything I mention must of course have occurred to me—an incomplete sampling is better than none at all.

Here, then, are some of the things that I think it is not impermissible to feel or think. It is, I maintain, not morally wrong to

1. Beam hatred at the elderly woman who is fumbling with her coupons and holding up the checkout line while your ice cream melts;
2. Be embarrassed by your spouse's grammatical lapses (bad posture, social gaffes, etc.);
3. Think, while consoling a friend who has received a bad diagnosis, "Better you than me";
4. Be pleased that a professional acquaintance who isn't as good as you has had a manuscript rejected;
5. Be pleased that a professional acquaintance who is better than you has had a manuscript rejected;
6. Find the painful pratfalls on *America's Funniest Home Videos* endlessly amusing;
7. Hope the plane whose landing you are watching catches a wing tip on the ground and cartwheels in a ball of fire; or
8. Wish someone you dislike would die.

And here are some beliefs—all false, many noxious—that I take similarly to escape moral condemnation. It is, I maintain, not morally wrong to believe that

9. The poor are just lazy;

10. The richest 1% (environmental criminals, Republicans, etc.) should be imprisoned and the worst of them shot;

11. Women (Blacks, Jews, etc.) are intellectually or morally inferior to others;

12. Men, with their rampant testosterone, are responsible for 90% of the world's troubles;

13. Women who dress provocatively are asking for it;

14. Six-year-olds can give meaningful consent and aren't harmed by sex anyhow;

15. Homosexuality is abnormal;

16. The act with the best consequences is always the right one to perform.

And here, finally, is a tiny sampling of the fantasies that I take to fall outside morality's purview. It is, I maintain, not wrong to fantasize about

17. Dropping a heavy object from the top of the Empire State Building;

18. Punching an obnoxious child;

19. Keying every Hummer (every Prius) in the parking lot;

20. Having sex with your married neighbor (your sister, the secretary of the treasury, a ruminant, etc.);

21. Having nonconsensual sex with any of the above;

22. Licking your own genitals, like a dog; or even

23. Dressing up as a clown to attract children to sodomize, dismember, and bury under your house.

Exercise for the reader: extend each list.

II

My claim that thoughts like these are not subject to moral condemnation appears to be a minority view. Because moral theorists are understandably preoccupied with what goes on in the public world, they do not often say much about purely private fantasies, emotions, and beliefs. However, when they do address such issues, they generally say things like this:

> Consider . . . a person who considers herself very progressive and liberal, but who discovers she is harboring serious prejudices against homosexuals. She might be unwilling to publicly express her attitudes precisely because she believes that they cannot be morally justified. In cases of this sort, I would argue, there might well be grounds for feeling guilty. . . . Morality may demand that we not harbor malicious, disrespectful, or prejudiced attitudes toward others, but [sic] this demand seems morally justifiable.[1]

> It is morally wrong to admire Hitler . . . it is morally wrong to delight at another person's suffering, it is morally right to be pleased by justice and disgusted with oppression, etc.[2]

> Imagine . . . an aging man who finds himself beset by persistent desires to rape a younger woman. It seems to me that this persistent longing is an occasion for a morally directed self-criticism and self-reform, and that this would remain true even if the man were entirely confident that he would never permit himself to rape anyone.[3]

Say that we are envious and unfairly resentful of our colleague's success in competition with us and driven by this to an intense dislike of him. Resentment, envy, detestation all determine what we are prepared to believe about him. We believe our colleague to be a fool because we *wish* he were a fool; we believe him merely lucky and probably corrupt because we *wish* him to be worthy of our contempt. Such believing is morally wrong because it is generated

---

[1] Angela Smith, "Guilty Thoughts," in Carla Bagnoli, ed., *Morality and the Emotions* (Oxford: Oxford University Press, 2011), p. 243.
[2] Alan Hazlett, "How to Defend Response Moralism," *British Journal of Aesthetics* 49, no. 3 (July 2009), p. 245.
[3] Talbot Brewer, *The Bounds of Choice: Unchosen Virtues, Unchosen Commitments* (New York: Garland, 2000), p. 38.

by sheer dislike of the man and this is a vicious way of determining belief.[4]

> The intuition that a joke can be funny even though it is wrong to be amused by it is, we think, quite powerful. . . . [Emotions such as amusement] may fit their object despite being wrong to feel. Indeed, we think this dictum holds of all basic emotions.[5]

Despite the diversity of their subject matter, these passages converge on the view that even purely private mental occurrences are fair game for moral assessment. That is the view I want to reject.

III

In taking this position, I do not mean to deny that a person's preoccupations and fantasies can reflect badly on his character. I fully acknowledge that it's not so nice to take pleasure in another's pain and that, past a certain point, the standard human foibles go decisively over into vice. I also have no wish to deny that beliefs that are unsupported by evidence can be criticized for their epistemic defects. My point is simply that where a person's private mental contents are concerned, these are the *only* forms of condemnation that are in place. There are certainly reasons not to be vicious or irrational, but these are not moral reasons. We will go badly astray if we take the further step of maintaining that it's *morally wrong* to have fantasies about molesting children, that it's *impermissible* to dwell on thoughts of grisly revenge, or that we are *morally obligated* to avoid beliefs that are rooted in prejudice rather than evidence.

Because I am placing a lot of weight on the distinction between moral reasons on the one hand and epistemic and aretaic reasons on the other, I want to make explicit the conception of morality that I take to underlie that distinction. As I see it, morality is a response

---

[4] Damien Cox and Michael Levine, "Believing Badly," *Philosophical Papers* 33, no. 3 (November 2004), p. 225.

[5] Justin D'Arms and Daniel Jacobson, "The Moralistic Fallacy: On the 'Appropriateness' of Emotions," *Philosophy and Phenomenological Research* 61, no. 1 (July 2000), pp. 80 and 82.

to certain basic facts about the human situation. Each of us is an embodied being who is surrounded by others like him, and each has both the capacity and the incentive to act in ways that adversely affect others. We all have many needs and wants that far outrun the available resources. We are soft and squishy and are adept at hurting each other. We communicate in a public language that makes it easy both to deceive and to wound. We regularly find ourselves in prisoner's dilemma situations in which we are collectively better off if we all cooperate but are individually better off if we defect while others cooperate. Because our situation is structured by these facts, we often have both the incentive and the opportunity to pursue our own interests at the expense of those of others. As reflective creatures, we therefore face questions about whether (and if so, how and to what degree) we should do so. As I understand them, the principles of common morality (and, by extension, the philosophical theories that seek either to ground or to alter them) are best regarded as attempts to answer this question from a suitably general point of view.

If this general approach is correct, then it follows immediately that moral reasons are distinct from epistemic ones, for if they were not, then morality would have no practical implications. The harder question, though, is why the needed practical directives should concern particular datable acts (and, on the view I oppose, thoughts) and not the broader traits of character from which these spring. A character trait is a disposition to think, feel, and act in certain characteristic ways, so if someone is sufficiently virtuous, he will act and think virtuously all the time. Thus, as long as people have compelling reasons to be fair, honest, and kind, there may appear to be little point in maintaining that they also have reasons of a different sort to manifest these virtues on particular occasions.

But on closer inspection, it is not so easy to dispense with the need for an independent class of moral reasons, for it is one thing to say that each person has good reason to be completely virtuous and quite another to say that each person in fact is. In the real world, even the best of us are often inclined to cut corners, preoccupied with our own concerns, and incapable of the effortless kindness, fairness, and honesty that a fully virtuous person would display. This doesn't mean that anyone is doomed to act badly, but it does mean that we all face innumerable occasions on which the question of how to reconcile our interests with those of others is not rendered otiose by our ingrained virtuous dispositions. This is precisely the question that a morality of obligation and permission is designed to answer. Thus, even if our most urgent task is to become the sort of people who naturally treat others fairly, honestly, and kindly, those of us who have not yet fully achieved this goal—that is, all of us—will still need the kind of rational guidance that only a morality can provide.

In the preceding paragraphs, I have relied on a description of morality's task that draws such facts as the unavoidable scarcity of resources, our mutual vulnerability, and the lack of congruence among different people's ambitions and aims. Because these are all facts about the public world, my claim that morality is a response to the problems they raise may appear to stack the deck against the view that its principles can apply even to private thoughts. However, on closer inspection, no deck-stacking has occurred; for even if morality's task is to regulate our interactions in the public world, it hardly follows that the only principles that can discharge that task are ones that apply exclusively to public behavior. It is indeed possible for morality to regulate our interactions by mandating only outward actions—that is a crude version of the view I favor—but it is also possible for morality to do this by imposing obligations and prohibitions that apply to the inner states from which our outward actions spring. Jesus appears to be expressing a view of the latter sort when he says

> Do you not see that whatever goes into the mouth enters the stomach, and goes out into the sewer? But what comes out of the mouth proceeds from the heart, and this is what defiles. For out of the heart come evil intentions, murder, adultery, fornication, theft, false witness, slander. These are what defile a person, but to eat with unwashed hands does not defile.[6]

Because a moral system may achieve its aim of regulating human behavior by constraining our actions, our thoughts, or both, the choice

---

[6] Matthew 15:17–20.

among these alternatives will have to be made on some further and more substantive basis.

IV

Morality, like the Pope, has no battalions. Even if certain beliefs or attitudes or fantasies are morally off limits, there is nothing that can stop us from having them. In the absence of an effective thought police, any moral restrictions on thought can be ignored with impunity. But if all such restrictions would be impotent, what's the point of asking whether any are defensible?

This question can be answered in more than one way. One good reason to inquire about the moral status of thoughts is simply to deepen our general understanding of what morality requires. Another is to find out how we, as particular individuals, must comport ourselves if we are to satisfy morality's requirements. Of these reasons, each is a staple of normative inquiry. Moreover, the second reason, far from being undermined by our ability to flout morality's requirements, is actually predicated on our *having* that ability.

There is, in addition, a further and more practical reason to ask whether morality's requirements extend as far as private thoughts: namely, to assess the rationale for a number of familiar practices that appear to be aimed precisely at expunging certain morally objectionable ideas from people's minds. A partial list of these practices would include mandatory diversity training, campaigns against books and films that objectify women, the ostracism of those who deny anthropogenic climate change, and the increasingly common use of the heckler's veto against speakers with retrograde views. Although some may support some of these practices for pragmatic reasons (e.g., as ways of promoting racial equality, preventing rape, or slowing global warming), there are many others who appear to support them on the simpler grounds that the targeted beliefs, attitudes, and fantasies are morally beyond the pale. If I am right in maintaining that no thoughts are morally impermissible, then all justifications of the latter sort will fail.

These reasons for investigating the moral status of thoughts are all important, but another is more important still. As I see it, the deepest reason for taking this question seriously is the threat that moralism about the mental poses to freedom of mind. We are all familiar with the argument that political censorship undermines freedom of thought;[7] but no less than someone who avoids a certain thought because he fears being found out and punished, someone who views that thought as morally off limits will not consider himself at liberty to think it, and so will to that extent be less free. From this perspective, it doesn't matter whether the person's reason for avoiding the heretical thought is his fear that the thought police will have him fired and brutalize his family or his own willing acceptance of a moral restriction. There is of course a vast difference between the two *sources* of unfreedom— the thought police are bad and blameworthy, the true morality presumably good and benign—but as long as they are equally effective in motivating avoidance of the forbidden thoughts, their impact on a person's freedom of mind will be essentially the same.

This last claim may seem overstated, in that decisions to internalize moral constraints on thought, unlike decisions made under threat, may themselves be genuine expressions of an agent's will. Kant argued, indeed, that autonomy consists precisely of giving oneself the moral law. However, to reconcile self-censorship with freedom in this way would be to blur the distinction between an agent's decision to internalize a prohibition against certain thoughts and whatever further movements of mind his unwillingness to think those thoughts prevents him from making.

For however free a person's acceptance of a prohibition on thought may be, the prohibition's inevitable effect is to diminish his *further* freedom by placing certain other thoughts off limits to him. This is easiest to see if we take his decision to accept the prohibition to antedate the self-censorship it requires; for in that case the difference between the two classes of thoughts is evident from their temporal separation. However, even if the decision to avoid a certain class of thoughts is not confined to any single time, but rather is continually renewed, each successive renewal will remain distinct from whatever further exercises of freedom it prevents. Thus, even if someone's decision to internalize a moral constraint on thought is every bit as free as the

[7] For a lucid recent treatment, see Seana Valentine Shiffrin, "A Thinker-Based Approach to Freedom of Speech," *Constitutional Commentary* 27, no. 2 (2011), pp. 283–307.

Kantians say it is, its impact on his mental freedom will remain deeply problematic.

My aim in highlighting this impact is not to argue that our thoughts *can't* be subject to moral regulation—that argument will come later—but is simply to point out that anyone who takes morality to limit what he may think will be forced to truncate the natural flow of his ideas in certain important ways. There will be various hypotheses that he will not be allowed to entertain, various possibilities that he will not be allowed to imagine, and various forms of solace of which he will not be allowed to avail himself. In the chapters to come, I will argue that these deformations of thought do give us reason to reject the thesis that would impose them, but for now it is enough to recognize that they would occur. Given the impact that moral constraints on thought would have on our mental lives, we surely have every reason to ask whether they are in fact called for.

V

As I've said, I think they're not, and my strategy in explaining why will be first to criticize the best available arguments for the constraints and then to make a positive case for rejecting them. However, before I get to any of that, I want briefly to mention, in order to dismiss, two superficially appealing arguments which, if correct, would render further discussion superfluous. Interestingly, one of these potential showstoppers is an argument against my view, while the other is an argument in its favor.

The argument that tells against my view is an appeal to the indisputable fact that many actions owe their moral status to features that extend well beyond the physical movements they involve. It is, for example, beyond doubt that whether someone violates the moral stricture against lying depends on whether he believes his utterance to be false; that harming someone maliciously is worse than harming him carelessly; and that shoving someone hard is blameworthy if done with hostility but praiseworthy if intended to prevent impact with an oncoming vehicle. In these and innumerable other cases, the nature and moral status of what we do cannot be read off our public behavior but rather is determined by the behavior's relation to states that can be kept purely private.[8] And from this, doesn't it follow immediately that the reach of morality does extend into the private realm?

The answer, I think, is that it does not follow; for what morality governs in these cases are not purely private occurrences but rather composite occurrences that have both public and private components. To warrant condemnation for maliciously injuring someone, a person must not only harbor the malice but actually inflict the injury. Thus, taken by itself, the claim that it is wrong to give public expression to private malice does not imply that there is anything wrong with simply entertaining the malice. To evaluate the latter claim, we cannot simply note the nonpublic elements of the activities that morality governs but must ask whether these elements retain their moral significance when we consider them in abstraction from their public sequelae.

The countervailing argument that I want to set aside is that private thoughts cannot be subject to moral regulation because thoughts are not actions and morality governs only actions. This argument draws support from various familiar facts: that we often cannot help believing what our evidence shows; that feelings such as fear, anger, and disgust follow automatically on certain beliefs; that many fantasies come into our minds unbidden; and so on. Nevertheless, although these facts are often taken to support the position I want to defend, I have several reasons for not relying on them.

One reason not to deploy this argument is that doing so would beg the question against my opponents, who are surely aware that believing, being amused, and having recurrent fantasies are not actions over which we exercise control, and who therefore evidently believe that morality's requirements *do* extend beyond such actions. My second reason for not pursuing it is that I tend to agree with my opponents on this point. I believe, for example, that it is sometimes appropriate to blame a person for an omission that reflects his failure to realize what he should do. When someone forgets to keep an appointment or doesn't notice that the baby is turning blue, his omission

---

[8] For discussion of the relation between a person's motives and the rightness or wrongness of his actions, see Steven Sverdlik, *Motive and Rightness* (Oxford: Oxford University Press, 2011).

is neither voluntary nor within his control. Thus, if such omissions can warrant moral condemnation, as I think they often can, then morality's requirements must extend beyond our voluntary actions and abstentions.[9]

My third reason for rejecting the argument that thoughts are not subject to moral regulation because they are not actions is that a good many private thoughts *do* qualify as actions. Although it is true that many thoughts come to us unbidden, it is also true that we exercise agency whenever we decide to set aside an intellectual puzzle that has been nagging at us, to continue wracking our brains for a name we cannot quite recall, or to go for a good wallow in a particularly scurrilous fantasy. Because we are fully capable of performing these and many other mental acts, the most that an appeal to agency could establish is that a smaller proportion of private thoughts than public actions are subject to moral evaluation and guidance. That is not a particularly interesting conclusion.

VI

But I think there are other and better reasons to deny that thoughts are subject to moral constraint, and I now want to present a brief overview of these. Because our topic is the relation between morality and private thought, we can approach it from either of two directions: first, by bringing what we know about morality to bear on its ability to regulate private thought and, second, by bringing what we know about private thought to bear on its ability to be regulated by morality. In the chapters that follow, I will advance arguments of both sorts.

One obvious impediment to beginning with what we know about morality is that so much of moral theory is disputed. Philosophers disagree both about what the basic principles of morality are (and, indeed, about whether morality is a matter of principle at all) and about how the true principles, whatever they are, can be justified. This does not

---

[9] For relevant discussion, see my *In Praise of Blame* (Oxford: Oxford University Press, 2006) and *Who Knew? Responsibility without Awareness* (Oxford: Oxford University Press, 2009).

mean that we cannot critically examine the case for taking morality to regulate the subjective realm, but it does mean that any such examination will require a discussion of several different classes of arguments.

Although thoughts themselves are private, they have important public effects, and these are not always benign. Thus, one obvious way to argue that a given belief, attitude, or fantasy is morally wrong is to draw attention to its bad consequences. Because judgments of moral wrongness can be either retrospective or prospective, this class of consequentialist arguments can itself be divided into two subclasses: one that moves backward from the present badness of a thought's consequences to the previous wrongness of the agent's having had the thought, and another that moves forward from the present likelihood that a thought will bring bad consequences to the current wrongness of the agent's having it. Despite their superficial similarity, these two kinds of consequentialist arguments raise very different issues.

Where arguments of the first, retrospective type are concerned, the central question is whether, and if so exactly how, the goodness or badness of what happens at a later time can retroactively affect the moral status of what came before. This question lies right at the border between ethics and metaphysics. By contrast, because the potential bad consequences with which the prospective arguments are concerned have not yet occurred, these arguments raise few(er) metaphysical issues but a broader range of questions of an empirical and normative nature. The main empirical questions concern the magnitudes of the risks that attach to particular beliefs, attitudes, and fantasies, while the main normative questions concern the levels of risk that individuals may permissibly impose on others. Because the two sets of issues are so different, I will devote most of Chapter 2 to the retrospective consequentialist arguments and the remainder of Chapter 2 and all of Chapter 3 to the prospective ones. Although it cannot be denied that some thoughts do raise the likelihood of harmful action—the obsessive fantasies of child molesters come immediately to mind—my tentative conclusion will be that the risks of harm they pose are never great enough to qualify as impermissible.

Despite its salience, the consequentialist approach is not a natural fit with the claim that some thoughts are morally off limits; for when people advance that claim, they are generally concerned less with a thought's consequences than with its content. What moralists about the mental really want to say is that certain beliefs, attitudes, and fantasies are morally impermissible simply in virtue of the kinds of thoughts they are. One way to flesh out this idea is to say that thoughts with certain contents are impermissible because they manifest a vicious character, while another is to say that they are impermissible because they violate moral rules that forbid such thoughts. Of these strategies, the first relies on attempts to understand rightness and wrongness in terms of what a virtuous person would or would not do (or, by extension, think), while the second exploits the justificatory machinery of one or another deontological theory to arrive at a set of moral prohibitions that apply to thoughts as well as acts.

These strategies will be addressed in Chapters 4 and 5. To assess the first, I will discuss the prospects for grounding prohibitions on thoughts in the main eudaemonistic and Platonistic variants of the virtue-theoretic approach, while to assess the second, I will discuss the prospects for grounding those prohibitions in the two deontological theories that are most prominently mentioned in this connection, those of Thomas Scanlon and of Kant himself. If each of these attempts fails, as I think each does, then the part of our discussion that begins with what we know about morality will end with the conclusion that its requirements are unlikely to extend into the subjective realm.

That conclusion is reinforced, moreover, when we come at things from the other end and draw on what we know about the subjective realm to ask how our lives will be affected if we *do* take our private thoughts to be subject to moral regulation. My answer to this question will consist of two claims: first, that when we wholeheartedly embrace the idea that certain beliefs, attitudes, or fantasies are morally off limits, we suffer a loss of mental freedom that extends far beyond an inability to entertain those particular thoughts; and, second, that any such loss will deprive us of much that is good and valuable, and thus will greatly impoverish our lives. This combination of claims is intended both as a counterweight to any as yet undefeated reasons to favor moralism about the mental and as a freestanding argument against it.

The threat to mental freedom that is posed by internalized constraints on thought is rooted in the fact that every belief, attitude, and fantasy is both associatively and inferentially connected to many others. No belief would persist if enough other supporting beliefs were removed; each attitude is rooted in a complex collection of empirical assumptions and deeper values; and each fantasy is triggered by associations that generally could not have been predicted in advance. Because the elements of our mental lives are so intertwined, anyone who seeks to avoid any given thought must also avoid many others. Thus, any moral prohibition that is targeted at any particular thought is bound to extend to many of the others that cause it, justify it, or render it appealing. Internalizing such a prohibition will therefore significantly restrict both the inquiries a person is willing to undertake and the unchosen flow of his ideas, and I will argue in Chapter 6 that these restrictions curtail his mental freedom in no less than four distinct ways.

Internalized prohibitions against theft, murder, and other public acts also limit our freedom, so this fact about internalized prohibitions against thoughts does not by itself set them apart. However, as I will argue in Chapter 7, the losses of freedom that accompany internalized restrictions on thought seem far less benign than those that accompany internalized restrictions on action. For one thing, because anyone who accepts a moral prohibition against a given thought must also be committed to resisting any others that would cause him to have it, prohibitions against thoughts are far more restrictive than prohibitions against actions. Also, and more subtly, internalized prohibitions on thoughts can be expected to alter the usual patterns of inference and other nonvoluntary processes that make us the persons we are. As a result, the bowdlerized thoughts that emerge will lack a certain authenticity: they will be less than full expressions of our rational nature and distinctive personality. By contrast, no such deformation occurs when an internalized restriction on outward behavior prevents someone from performing an action without affecting either his inclination to perform it or any of the deeper processes that give rise to that inclination.

I believe that each of these effects represents a significant cost and that, taken together, those costs are high enough to justify a complete repudiation of all restrictions on thought. However, I also believe that even together, the cited costs do not come close to exhausting the field. A very different reason to resist restrictions on thought, less philosophically interesting but more humanly compelling, is that only complete mental freedom can fully secure both the joys and the consolations of privacy. If there are thoughts that are so bad that we must not think them, then we can experience neither the exhilaration that accompanies the frictionless free play of the imagination nor the solace of a redoubt that is ours and ours alone. My belief in the human necessity of these possibilities is the emotional engine that drives my argument, and I will try to give it expression in the book's concluding sections. There and throughout, my paradoxical aim will be to give the reader intellectual permission to think a thought that—like every other thought—he is in reality free to think without asking permission.

2

Harmful Thoughts

Our thoughts are all private in the sense that we alone have direct access to them, but they are *not* all private in the sense of never impinging on the public world. To the contrary, each person's thoughts regularly shape his actions, and those actions regularly affect others, often in harmful ways. Because every moral system contains prohibitions against harming, it may seem obvious that every moral system must also prohibit at least some harmful thoughts. However, in the current chapter and the next, I will argue that this claim is neither obvious nor true.

I

Thoughts can lead to harm in more than one way, and we cannot assume that each causal pattern raises the same issues. Thus, before I turn to matters of substance, I must say something about the different causal pathways that run from private thoughts to public harms. I will distinguish four such pathways, two involving voluntary action and two not.

1. The most obvious way in which our thoughts can lead to harm is by giving us reasons to *act* harmfully. The claim that someone has a reason to act is notoriously ambiguous, in that it can mean either that he has at least a pro tanto justification for acting as he does or that his acting that way is motivated, and so explained, by some combination of his desires, beliefs, and other mental states. However, given our current focus on the causal paths from thought to harm, we need only consider reasons of the second, motivating sort. If a person's justifying reasons enter at all, it is only by contributing to his motivating reasons.

   When philosophers try to specify a person's reason for acting, they often do so exclusively in terms of desire and belief. Crudely

A Wild West of the Mind. George Sher, Oxford University Press (2021). © Oxford University Press.
DOI: 10.1093/oso/9780197564677.003.0002

put, the standard way of explaining why a person does A is to say that he both (1) wants something X and (2) believes that doing A is the only or best way of bringing X about. Whether this schema can accommodate explanations that mention attitudes, fantasies, and other mental states depends on whether claims about those other states can be analyzed into claims about beliefs and desires; but whether or not they can, our attitudes and fantasies are clearly among the factors that affect our motivation. Where our attitudes are concerned, this is easy to see—if we despise someone, we are motivated to avoid him, if we trust someone, we are willing to confide in him, and so on—but even our fantasies, though often idle, can sometimes stir us to action. Even when we don't fully understand our own motivation, the harms we are moved to bring about are often inflicted voluntarily.

2. People's ultimate aims differ greatly, but one intermediate aim that we all share is that of communicating our thoughts. When a thought motivates its own disclosure, the awareness of its content that it elicits is not only an effect but also a representation of that content. Eliciting such representations, moreover, is important to us for both tactical and emotional reasons: tactically because what others believe about our beliefs, desires, and attitudes is often crucial in determining how they will act, emotionally because we often care deeply about what others think of us. Although we can of course harm others by misrepresenting our thoughts, we can also do so by representing them accurately. We can do so by not bothering to conceal our disdain, by disclosing the contents of beliefs that will lead others to act destructively, and in many other ways. Although harming people by communicating our thoughts is of course a special case of harming them by acting, the role that communication plays in our interpersonal dealings is central enough to justify assigning it a separate category.

3. When others become aware of what is going on in our minds, the reason is generally that we have disclosed our thoughts voluntarily. However, even when we do our best to keep our thoughts to ourselves, they are sometimes discernible from the play of our facial expressions, our inflections, our tone of voice, or our choice of words. This involuntary leakage can itself result in hurt feelings

and harmful behavior, so it represents a third causal route from private thought to public harm.

4. But neither, finally, are intentional disclosure and behavioral tells the only possible sources of information about a person's thoughts and feelings. Even if someone is both secretive and very good at not betraying his thoughts, it is theoretically possible for others to gain access to them through some form of telepathy. That is what some mediums claim to be able to do, and their claim does not seem incoherent (although I would be shocked if it were true). Also, even if there are no telepaths, future advances in brain science may at some point enable investigators to infer what is going on in people's minds from their distinctive patterns of neural activity. Either way, what is learned may again have a harmful effect both on other people's feelings and on their subsequent behavior.

Here, then, are four different ways in which a person's private thoughts can indirectly lead to harm. But which of them, if any, might support the implication that it is wrong for him simply to *have* the harmful thoughts?

II

The answer, I think, is "none"; but because the four causal pathways are so different, my reasons are not the same in each case. Thus, to defend my answer, I will have to discuss each pathway separately.

Let's begin with thoughts that motivate harmful acts, and let's take as our illustration a long-standing grudge that erupts into petty vandalism. The star of our little drama is Solenz, an otherwise unexceptional suburbanite who loathes his next-door neighbor, Putterbaugh. Solenz's complaints about Putterbaugh are legion: he resents the man's flashy car, feels menaced by his leer, abhors his politics, is irritated by his postnasal drip, and can't stand the way he overpronounces his hard consonants. Eager for a confrontation but too timid to provoke one, Solenz quietly tips over Putterbaugh's wheelie bin on garbage day.

Inconveniencing your neighbor by tipping over his wheelie bin is wrong, and the causal sequence that leads to this particular tipping has its origins in Solenz's hostile thoughts. Hence, at least to this extent, those thoughts are implicated in Solenz's wrong act. But does this mean that his thinking them is itself wrong? Does the wrongness of the bin-tipping flow backward to the hostile thoughts that have motivated it? Can we infer, from the fact that Solenz would not have tipped over the bin if he had not had the hostile thoughts, that it was wrong for him to have the thoughts as well as to tip the bin?

An act's wrongness obviously cannot infect *every* previous event in whose absence it would not have occurred: the wrongness of a lie does not make it wrong to be born with vocal cords. But given the close connections between the things that people do and the reasons for which they do them, it is less implausible to suppose that an act's wrongness might flow back at least as far as the beliefs and attitudes on which it was based. Moreover, plausible or not, it is hard to see how anyone could take the wrongness of a public act to establish the wrongness of the private thoughts that lead to it without saying something along these lines.[1] For both reasons, it is worth pointing out that this view—I'll call it the flow-back view—is problematic on at least three counts.

Perhaps the most obvious difficulty is that even when two people share the same deplorable attitudes, the flow-back view implies that their attitudes need not be equally wrong.[2] If what makes someone's private attitude wrong is the backwash from the public acts to which it leads, then even if two people have equally deplorable private attitudes, their having them will not be equally wrong if one but not the other is moved by his attitude to *do* something wrong.[3] Moreover, if the

---

[1] One philosopher who appears to hold this view is Earl Spurgin, who writes that "[a]ny moral state, whether it is an emotion, fantasy, belief, attitude, or any other type, is subject to moral condemnation if it is part of a causal chain that produces an immoral act. If a person commits a racist act, it is appropriate to condemn morally not only the act, but, also, the person's racist beliefs that helped produce the act." Earl Spurgin, "An Emotional-Freedom Defense of *Schadenfreude,*" *Ethical Theory and Moral Practice* 18 (2015), p. 782.

[2] Spurgin recognizes this implication but doesn't appear to view it as an objection. Speaking of a man who is pleased by the death of his ex-wife's new husband, he writes that "the fact that he experiences that emotion gives us no reason to condemn it morally. If Joe were to attend the man's funeral or memorial service and share his pleasure with the man's friends and family, however, then we have reason to condemn morally his emotion" ("A Freedom-Based Defense of *Schadenfreude,*" p. 783).

[3] One thing that might explain why only one of the two people acts on his deplorable attitude is that only one of them has the *opportunity* to do so. If we focus exclusively on cases like this, we may be tempted to suppose that the objection is simply that the flow-back view commits us to the existence of circumstantial moral luck. However, if that were the problem, then the objection would have no force for those who are sympathetic to moral luck, as I in fact am, and it would not arise at all in cases in which both agents

attitude that moves an agent to act wrongly at time t lies dormant until t, then his having the attitude before t will not be wrong before t, but his having had the attitude before t *will* be wrong *after* t. The flowback view has this paradoxical implication because a person's beliefs, attitudes, and fantasies generally antedate any wrong acts to which they lead, and so can be made wrong by those acts only through some form of backward normative influence.

A second problem with the flow-back view is that it proves too much. Resentment and hostility are unattractive attitudes, so there may be some initial appeal to the supposition that having them can be made wrong by the wrongness of the actions to which they lead. However, as I have argued elsewhere, the private occurrences that lead agents to act wrongly need not be unattractive, but can be combinations of beliefs, desires, and attitudes each of which is either neutral or positively desirable. Here is one example from that earlier work:

> Alphonse is a generous and empathetic person, but he is also a tormented soul. He is someone who feels compromised by even unintended lapses from moral perfection, who judges himself extremely harshly, and who tends to express his harsh judgment in self-destructive ways. Knowing that he is prone to downward spirals, Alphonse tries scrupulously to do the right thing. However, on one occasion, he unwittingly acquires a piece of information he should not have and, though in fact blameless, predictably begins to feel worthless and anomic. Acting in a spirit of moral self-defilement, Alphonse makes a cruel remark of precisely the kind that he most abhors.[4]

Because it is wrong for Alphonse to make his cruel remark, the flowback view implies that it was also wrong for him to have the attitudes of

have had the opportunity to act on their deplorable attitudes. But in fact, the objection does arise in such cases; for even when both agents are assumed to have had the same opportunities, it remains counterintuitive to suppose that the difference in what they actually did can make a retroactive difference to the moral status of their earlier attitudes.

[4] This example originally appeared in George Sher, *In Praise of Blame* (Oxford: Oxford University Press, 2006), pp. 23–24.

generosity and conscientiousness whose interaction led him to make it.[5] But this implication is hard to swallow: having generous and conscientious attitudes is surely not wrong.

The last problem I will mention concerns the flow-back view's account of the relation between a person's private thoughts and the public actions to which they give rise. To say that the wrongness of a public action flows backward to the beliefs, attitudes, or fantasies that have motivated it, we must assume that the route from them to it was both causal and direct. However, although the route is indeed likely to have been causal, it can hardly have been direct; for when a person's beliefs, attitudes, fantasies, and the rest lead him to act, they do so by providing him with reasons for a decision that lies *between* them and the act. Such decisions are not always conscious, and any attempt to spell out what they involve would quickly embroil us in mysteries, but any transition from a mere set of private beliefs, attitudes, and the like to a reason-based public action must clearly be mediated by some kind of agency. Because the causal path from a set of beliefs, attitudes, and fantasies to a public action must always runs through a decision that is made by the agent, the natural earliest point back to which the wrongness of an action can flow is not the agent's beliefs, attitudes, and fantasies themselves, but rather his decision to act for the reasons he takes them to provide.

III

Yet even if a person's private beliefs, attitudes, and fantasies are insulated from the wrongness of his actions by the decisions that stand between them, the same cannot be said of another class of purely

---

[5] Jan-Willem Wieland has raised the possibility of blocking this objection by maintaining that an act's wrongness flows back to the agent's motivating desire only when that desire's propositional object matches the act's wrong-making features. If the flow-back view is qualified in this way, then it will imply that the cruelty of Alphonse's remark does *not* flow back to any of the benign thoughts whose interaction has motivated the remark. However, although a proponent of the flow-back view will presumably welcome this implication, he will presumably be less pleased by the further implication that the wrongness of Alphonse's remark also will not flow back if his motivating desire was not to inflict suffering but rather to aggrandize himself or intimidate the other students.

private states. The states I have in mind are intentions, and the crucial fact about them is that they can exist only *after* agents have decided to act. A person's intending to do something is just as conclusive an indication that he has decided to do it as is his actually doing it. Moreover, when a decision does issue in an intention rather than action, the explanation lies not in any lesser degree of commitment on the part of the agent, but only in the fact that he either cannot do the thing right away or else has some reason to wait. But if intentions are this closely connected to the actions that morality paradigmatically regulates—if their function is simply to freeze an agent's post-decision readiness to act until it is possible or convenient for him to do so—then shouldn't they have the same moral status as the actions themselves? If it is wrong to do something, then isn't it also wrong to harbor a private intention to do it?[6]

That the answer may be "yes" is suggested not only by what was just said but also by the fact that unsuccessful attempts to perform wrong acts are not rendered innocent by their failure. Philosophers may disagree about whether trying to murder someone is *as* wrong as actually doing so, but not about whether they are both wrong. It seems, moreover, that what the two have in common, and what explains *why* they are both wrong, is that they both stem from decisions to perform wrong acts. However, if an act that stems from a decision to do something wrong can be wrong for reasons independent of its success in bringing about the intended outcome, then why shouldn't a private intention that stems from such a decision also be wrong for reasons independent of its success in bringing about the intended outcome?

There is, to be sure, a well-entrenched legal doctrine which asserts that agents shouldn't be punished for intentions on which they have not publicly acted. Legal punishment, it is said, always requires an act. However, the view of legal culpability that underlies this doctrine will

---

[6] If it's wrong to intend to do what it's wrong to do, then nuclear deterrence is almost certainly impermissible; for it seems that in order to be effective, a deterrent threat must be backed by a genuine intention to perform the quintessentially wrong act of incinerating millions of innocent people if their leaders use nuclear weapons first. For discussion, see Douglas Maclean, ed., *The Security Gamble: Deterrence Dilemmas in the Nuclear Age* (Totowa, NJ: Rowman and Allanheld, 1984), especially the essays by Hehir, Sher, Gauthier, Kavka, and Lewis.

only carry over to the moral context if the best justification for it also carries over, and that does not appear to be the case. To see the point of the legal doctrine, we need only remind ourselves that legal punishment must be based on convincing evidence, and that evidence of unmanifested intentions is hard to come by. This suggests that the reason the law refuses to criminalize purely private intentions is simply that that would create a class of crimes for whose commission the state could rarely obtain convincing evidence.[7] If the law's refusal to punish people for unmanifested intentions is rooted in an evidential requirement that morality does not share, as I think is the case, then it will not undermine the claim that the unmanifested intentions can be morally wrong.

But there is another consideration that is more effective at undermining the parallel between unsuccessful attempts and unmanifested intentions, and that is the fact that from an attempt, but not an intention, there is no going back. Once the hit man has pulled the trigger, the success of his attempt is (literally) out of his hands. At that point, whether the victim dies no longer depends on him, but instead depends on such factors as the path of the bullet, the victim's exact movements, and the presence or absence of intervening objects. Once the hit man has actually made his attempt (as opposed to merely taking steps toward making it), he has fully done his part, and that's what he deserves to be punished for.

But the situation is very different if someone merely *intends* to do something wrong, for in that case it does remain possible for him to change his mind, and so the outcome is not yet out of his hands. It is a striking and important fact that our present decisions can never bind our future selves. No matter how resolute we are in forming an intention, we can never foreclose the possibility that we will see things differently at some point before we act. The only way to ensure that we will act on our current intentions is to make arrangements (tying ourselves to the mast, pouring the liquor down the drain, pledging to eat

---

[7] For argument along these lines, see Gideon Yaffe, *Attempts* (Oxford: Oxford University Press, 2010), ch. 8. For an interestingly different explanation of the law's refusal to criminalize unmanifested intentions, which also is consistent with the idea that intentions can be morally wrong, see Herbert Morris, "Punishment for Thoughts," in his *On Guilt and Innocence* (Berkeley: University of California Press, 1976), pp. 1–29.

something disgusting if we don't follow through) that make it impossible or inordinately difficult to do otherwise. And to do anything like this is of course *already* to act on one's current intention.

Because a mere intention can never rule out a change of heart, there is a clear sense in which anyone who acts on a preexisting intention is making a further decision not to go back on his earlier decision. Because it is this last decision that actually initiates his action, the earlier intention is no part of the sequence that runs from the initiating decision to the action. Thus, if it is the initiating decision that insulates the person's private states from the wrongness of his action, then the states that it seals off include not only his desires, beliefs, and attitudes, but also whichever intentions *preceded* the initiating decision. Even if everything that happens after the initiating decision is subject to moral evaluation, the merely private intentions that precede it are not. Thus, despite their orientation to action, those intentions pose little threat to my claim that the private mental realm is morality-free.

IV

So far, I have discussed only the first of our four patterns of interaction, in which the relation between a private thought and its harmful public effects is specified exclusively in causal terms. But what, next, of the second pattern, in which that relation is representational as well as causal? How, if at all, is the normative situation altered when a thought causes harm by motivating the person who has it to communicate its content to others?

Most people care about what others think of them. If we find out that an acquaintance doesn't like or respect us (has sick fantasies about us, finds us repulsive, values us only as a means), we may react with anything from mild disappointment to suicidal despair, and our reaction is likely to be more intense if the other is a close friend or lover. In addition, an increasing number of people find the expression of an increasing number of opinions increasingly upsetting; and while I think the trend of trying to suppress any opinions that one finds upsetting is extremely dangerous, I see no reason to deny that the upset is often genuine. Also, quite apart from this, people regularly draw on their knowledge of what others think and feel in deciding what they themselves should do, and the decisions they reach on this basis can lead them to perform any number of further harmful acts.

These facts remind us that even if disclosing one's thoughts is not wrong in itself, causing harm by doing so may well be. Suppose, for instance, that my tongue has been loosened by alcohol or intimacy, and I impulsively blurt out what's really on my mind—"Nobody can stand your daughter," say, or "You people care too much for money" or "You have a funny smell." Because I am here expressing a thought that predictably wounds or offends you, it is not unreasonable to say that I am doing something wrong. Yet even if this is so, we are hardly warranted in taking the wrongness of my disclosing the thought to show that I was also wrong in thinking it. To see why we should not take this further step, we need only recall what was said about the parallel case of the aggrieved neighbor.

For when we asked whether the wrongness of Solenz's tipping over the wheelie bin flows back to the hostile thoughts that motivated his act, we found that any such conclusion would have a number of highly unpalatable implications. That inference would have to be grounded in a principle that treated thoughts with identical contents differently, would have paradoxical implications about the time at which a private thought becomes wrong, would imply that even benign private thoughts are sometimes wrong, and would ignore the mediating role of decisions in the causal sequences that run from thought to action. For all of these same reasons, we must now also reject the claim that the wrongness of a person's harmful disclosures flows back to the thoughts whose contents are disclosed. At least when a thought's disclosure is voluntary, the fact that the agent is wrong to disclose its contents does not support the conclusion that he is also wrong to think it.

V

But what, finally, of our remaining two patterns of interaction—the ones in which the contents of a person's thoughts are *not* voluntarily disclosed, but rather are either gleaned from behavioral clues or else discovered through telepathy or the decoding of neural activity? In each such case, whatever harm might result from the discovery of the person's thoughts is due not to his own actions but to the inferences or actions of others. In this way, his exposure to moral censure is in one way reduced. However, precisely because his thoughts are vulnerable to discovery in these ways, he may be under an obligation to take steps to conceal them, and so his moral exposure may in another way be increased. Because the most effective way to prevent the discovery of a potentially harmful thought is simply not to think it, this new obligation, if it exists, may itself support the conclusion that thinking certain thoughts is wrong.

The first thing to note about this proposal is that it involves a radical shift in perspective. In order to infer the wrongness of a thought from either the wrongness of the actions to which it leads or the harm that its disclosure causes, one must treat the events that follow upon the thought as fixed, and so must consider it from a retrospective point of view. By contrast, to infer the wrongness of a thought from the fact that it is *vulnerable* to discovery by others, one must assume that the ensuing events are not yet fixed, but rather may themselves be affected by what the agent does and does not think. Hence, to argue for the wrongness of a given thought on the grounds that it may become public and thereby lead to harm, one must consider the thought from a prospective or ex ante point of view.

To condemn a private thought on the grounds that it may cause harm if it becomes public is to imply that the risk of this outcome is unacceptably high. Whether that risk is unacceptable will depend, among other things, on the magnitude (or range of possible magnitudes) of each potential harm, the probability of each such harm, and the countervailing importance to the agent of being able to think thoughts of that kind. I believe, in fact, that the likelihood that others will gain seriously harmful knowledge of our thoughts from our facial expressions, body language, and the like is never high enough to make it wrong for us to think those thoughts. (Others evidently agree: no one, as far as I know, has argued that it is wrong to think any thought because it poses such a risk.) I also believe that we are never obligated to avoid any thoughts because they increase our risk of *acting* wrongly. However, because both of these claims raise complicated issues, I will defer any defense of them until the next chapter, which will be devoted entirely to the topic of moral hazard.

VI

Yet even if everything I say in that chapter is correct, it will not settle the question of whether it can be wrong to have thoughts to which others might gain access by telepathy or through the decoding of one's brain activity. The problem about these modes of access is not that they currently reveal much about anyone's thoughts—they clearly do not— but rather that they occupy a nether world that lies somewhere between fact and speculation. Because these forms of mind-reading are at present largely conjectural,[8] and because they can be envisioned as yielding anything from rough hints to fully specific information about what someone is thinking, there is no determinate risk of harm that a person's making himself vulnerable to them can be said to inflict on others.

Given our current inability to read people's minds or extract the details of their beliefs, attitudes, or fantasies from what we know about their brain-states, one way to deal with these possibilities is simply to dismiss them as irrelevant. However, even if we are not impressed by such flights of philosophical fancy as teletransportation and people-spores, we must at least acknowledge that no adequate reconstruction of morality can avoid telling us what we should do in some merely possible cases. If only because every actual situation is different from every other, any acceptable set of moral principles will have to provide us with guidance in some range of situations that we have not yet encountered. Moreover, even if we dismiss the possibility of telepathy on the grounds that we have neither any evidence that it occurs nor any idea of how it *could* occur, we cannot similarly dismiss the possibility of inferring the contents of people's thoughts from what is

---

[8] For discussion of the current state of research, see Marc J. Blitz, *Searching Minds by Scanning Brains: Neuroscience Technology and Constitutional Privacy Protection* (Cham, Switzerland: Palgrave Macmillan, 2017), ch. 3.

going on in their brains. It is already possible to correlate patterns of brain activity with moods, so keeping a poker face is not quite the defense against others becoming aware of our despair or elation that it once was. As brain science progresses, we can expect that ever more finely articulated reconstructions of the contents of people's subjectivities will become available.

Yet even if it became possible to discover exactly what others are thinking, it would, for the foreseeable future, remain easy enough to shield our incriminating beliefs, attitudes, and fantasies. To gain detailed information about the contents of a person's subjectivity, an investigator would have to (1) secure that person's cooperation with (2) trained personnel using (3) specialized equipment that is (4) in reasonably close proximity to him. As long as all this remains true, anyone who wishes to keep his thoughts to himself can do so by simply keeping his distance or withholding his cooperation from investigators. Just as we can keep our laptops private by angling our screens or not booting up until we leave Starbucks, we will be able to keep our thoughts private by denying others access to the information from which their contents could be inferred.[9] Thus, although continued progress in decoding the contents of thoughts may give rise to new obligations to block access to them, it poses no immediate threat to the view that they are exempt from moral regulation.

But things would get more complicated if the technology became less cumbersome and more readily available. Extrapolating from current trends, we can assume that any required equipment will become both smaller and less expensive. If devices capable of disclosing the contents of specific beliefs, attitudes, and fantasies could be miniaturized—if, say, they became as easy to conceal as the devices that can now steal information from unprotected passports—then concealing our thoughts would be much more difficult. If that happened, the legal system would almost certainly respond by banning the devices; and while the ban's main aim would be to protect our thoughts from harmful others, an incidental benefit would be to protect others from our harmful thoughts. As long as our social institutions kept pace with the evolving

---

[9] This analogy was suggested to me by Tim Schroeder.

technology, the harms that our private thoughts could do if they became public would not give us moral reason not to think them.

But it is also possible that our social institutions would not keep pace, and here, finally, the moral importance of the public/private distinction would begin to break down. If we were transparent to others, our thoughts would be as public as our actions, and so, like them, would be subject to moral constraints.[10] Or, at least, our thoughts would be subject to moral constraints if the conditions under which morality is possible continued to exist at all.

There is an episode of *Gilligan's Island* in which first Gilligan, and then the other inhabitants of the island, come into possession of some seeds that enable them to read one another's minds. The entirely predictable consequence is that everyone is offended by, and so becomes hostile toward, everyone else. In the sitcom the inhabitants are rescued from social breakdown when Gilligan wisely burns the plant that bears the seeds, but in a world in which things are not wrapped up in the twenty-sixth minute, the issue would not end as well. Whether anything like a morality could survive if everyone's thoughts and motives were fully transparent to everyone else is anybody's guess, and so too are the forms of social interaction that would develop in place of the current practices of strategic calculation that rely on concealment. In any event, because morality as we know it is a response to questions that arise in a world in which thoughts can be kept private, we approach the outer limits of coherence when we ask what it would require in a world in which they cannot.

---

[10] For discussion of some relevant ethical issues, see Adina L. Roskies, "Mind Reading, Lie Detection, and Privacy," in J. Clausen and Neil Levy, eds., *Handbook of Ethics* (Dordrecht: Springer, 2015), pp. 679–95.

3

Moral Risk

Are any thoughts too risky to be morally permissible? This question was left unresolved in the preceding chapter, and I want to return to it here. Reduced to its essentials, my answer will be that the risks that are posed by most thoughts do not even approach the permissibility threshold, but that a few of them do come close. In the end, I believe that none actually crosses the line, but because a risk's permissibility depends in part on what would be lost by not imposing it, I can't fully defend this claim without addressing the costs of self-censorship. Thus, the final step of my argument must await the positive case for freedom of mind that will be developed later in the book.

I

To determine whether a given risk is one that an agent may permissibly impose, we must consider (at least) the magnitude of the potential harm, its ex ante probability, the permissibility of inflicting it, and the magnitude of the burden of avoiding it.[1] Where the risk is posed by a private belief, attitude, or fantasy, the main burden associated with its avoidance is the loss of mental freedom that I have just mentioned and will say more about later. However, for now, what needs emphasis is simply that this burden will turn out to be significant across all the cases that interest us.

---

[1] On the simplest account, imposing a risk is permissible as long as the burden of avoiding the harm is greater than the magnitude of the harm as discounted by its (un) likelihood, while more complicated accounts either attach varying weights to these factors or else introduce others (such as whether the persons who would undergo the risks are also the ones who would bear the burden of avoiding them). For an interesting overview of the possibilities, see Kenneth Simons, "Negligence," *Social Philosophy and Policy* 16, no. 2 (Summer 1999), pp. 52–93.

A Wild West of the Mind. George Sher, Oxford University Press (2021). © Oxford University Press.
DOI: 10.1093/oso/9780197564677.003.0003

By contrast, before we can ask how the risks posed by thoughts fare in the other dimensions, we must make some distinctions. For one thing, there are several kinds of harm that thoughts can bring, so before we can assess the risk that is posed by any given thought, we must be clear about the kind(s) of harm we have in mind. In addition, as we saw in the preceding chapter, a thought can lead to harm in a number of ways, and the differences among these may also affect both the magnitude of the risk and the moral acceptability of imposing it.

Let's begin with the idea of harm itself. To say that someone has been harmed is to say (at least) that he has been made less well off in relation to some baseline.[2] Thus, any account of harm must presuppose some view of when a person *is* well or badly off. On just about any account, a person's well-being is lowered when he is physically injured or suffers a serious financial loss. In the view of many, he is also made worse off when his feelings are seriously hurt or he is deeply offended. In addition, on one popular philosophical account (which in good measure draws its support from its ability to accommodate judgments like the ones just mentioned), a person's level of well-being depends on the degree to which his desires are satisfied or frustrated. Corresponding to these familiar views about well-being, we can distinguish a number of different routes from thought to harm.

The most direct route corresponds to the third of the views just mentioned. If a person's well-being is reduced whenever his desires are frustrated, then one person can worsen another's situation simply by thinking of him as he prefers not to be thought of.[3] If you value your reputation as a philosopher, I can make you worse off by thinking you are a bad philosopher; if you prefer not to be the object of my fantasies,

[2] This formula is of course ridiculously oversimplified. For someone who wants to see how much complexity is packed into the notion of harm, a good place to start is Joel Feinberg, *Harm to Others* (Oxford: Oxford University Press, 1986). This work is part of a four-volume quadrilogy, entitled *The Moral Limits of the Criminal Law*, which is devoted entirely to sympathetic criticism and elaboration of John Stuart Mill's principle that the only acceptable justification for state interference with anyone's liberty is to prevent that person from harming others.

[3] For two articulations of the view that we can harm someone simply by having thoughts about him that he doesn't want us to have, see Simon Keller, "Belief for Someone Else's Sake," *Philosophical Topics* 46, no. 1 (Spring 2018), pp. 19–35, and Meir Dan-Cohen, *Harmful Thoughts* (Princeton, NJ: Princeton University Press, 2002), pp. 184–85.

I can harm you simply by fantasizing about you. In each case, you don't have to know about my thoughts to be made worse off by them; what matters is only their lack of congruence with the propositional objects of your desires. Because that lack of congruence is not causally mediated, the risk that one person's thoughts will harm another in this way depends not on the likelihood that any causal sequence will play itself out, but only on the likelihood that the other has desires that those thoughts would frustrate.

The second route from thought to harm—the one that corresponds to the harms of hurt feelings and offense—is quite different. We can be hurt or offended only by thoughts of which we are aware, so this kind of harm does require causal interaction. The harmful thought's disclosure may be either voluntary or involuntary, but either way, the person it is about (or, in some cases, some other person) must be made aware of it. Thus, where this kind of harm is concerned, the magnitude of the risk depends not only on the likelihood that the other will be offended if he finds out what we are thinking, but also on the likelihood that something will *cause* him to find out.

The third and final route from thought to harm—the one that corresponds to the harms of bodily injury and financial loss (and, we may add, setbacks to various aims and projects)—is different again; for to inflict a harm of this kind, an agent must do more than just reveal the content of his thoughts. In addition or instead, those thoughts must move him to act in a way that *leads* to some kind of injury, loss, or setback. A person's thoughts can lead him to inflict such harms in countless ways: he may write his children out of his will because he thinks they are unworthy, throw a punch (cause an accident, tip over a wheelie bin) because he is furious, bump into someone because he is lost in fantasy, and so on without end. Also, of course, he may be moved to do something that leads a third party to act harmfully. In each case, the risk that a given thought will lead to harm is the product of the likelihoods that (1) the thought will issue in some potentially harmful act and that (2) that act will in fact cause harm.

To assess the claim that some thoughts are too risky to be morally permissible, we will have to examine all three possible routes from thought to harm. Because the risk in each case depends on a different set of likelihoods, each route must be considered separately. I will discuss them in the order in which they were introduced.

II

Each of us knows hundreds if not thousands of people, and it is reasonable to assume that many of them care about our good opinion. It is also reasonable to assume that we don't *have* a good opinion of each. We consider some people unattractive, some pusillanimous and self-involved, some silly, some evil, and some (to enlist Rosalind Hursthouse's wonderful term) weak-minded. If people are made worse off simply by not getting what they want, and if many of whom we think badly want us *not* to think badly of them, then each censorious thought risks harming someone. As far as I know, no philosopher has invoked this risk to argue that it is wrong to have censorious thoughts. But what, exactly, would be wrong with arguing that way?

One thing that might be wrong, of course, is that the desire-satisfaction theory might not be true, while another is that the harm of being badly thought of might be so minor as always to be outweighed by other considerations or simply not worth talking about. It seems to me, however, that neither diagnosis is fully satisfactory. Although there are well-known reasons to restrict the desires whose satisfaction can count toward a person's well-being,[4] I think some trimmed-back versions of the desire-satisfaction theory, including some that allow a person's well-being to be affected by satisfactions or frustrations of which he isn't aware, are pretty plausible.[5] I think, as well, that the resulting reductions in well-being cannot always be dismissed as insignificant. If someone's reputation means everything to him, then his being a secret laughing-stock is no minor matter. Thus, if there is no better reason to reject the argument that censorious thoughts pose unacceptable risks of harm, then maybe we *shouldn't* reject it.

---

[4] For influential discussion of some relevant considerations, see James Griffin, *Well-Being* (Oxford: Oxford University Press, 1986), chs. 1 and 2.

[5] However, for defense of the opposing view that our desires affect our well-being only when we *believe* they're satisfied or frustrated, see Christopher Heathwood, "Desire Satisfaction and Hedonism," *Philosophical Studies* 128, no. 3 (April 2006), pp. 539–63.

But, in fact, there is a better reason, and it emerges as soon as we turn our attention from the harms that censorious thoughts can bring to the question of whether it is wrong to risk inflicting those harms. In general, it is wrong to risk inflicting a given type of harm only if actually inflicting such a harm would also be wrong. Thus, if it is wrong to risk harming people by frustrating their desires, then actually inflicting that kind of harm must also be wrong. But is it? Are we in fact obligated to avoid harming people simply by frustrating their desires?

It is hard to see how we could be, for given both the vast number of people whose desires can be satisfied or frustrated by any person's actions and the variety and heterogeneity of the desires that every person has, even the most ordinary of actions will often frustrate some people's strongly held desires. When I buy the last bulb of garlic, I may thwart the ambitions of the next shopper who is planning an important dinner; when I laugh at your joke, I may infuriate the nearby misanthrope who wants everyone to be miserable; when I succeed or fail, I may frustrate your desire that I fail or succeed. In these contexts and innumerable others, it isn't wrong—not even a little bit—for me to do what I do. Moreover, it wouldn't be any more wrong if there were hundreds of shoppers clamoring for garlic, thousands of misanthropes upset by jocularity, or millions of well- or ill-wishers rooting for my success or failure.

Because even the actual frustration of these desires would not make my action wrong, my merely risking their frustration cannot be wrong either. Moreover, there is, in this regard, little difference between desires that are frustrated by actions and desires that are frustrated by thoughts. Just as even the most ordinary of actions can frustrate the desires of any number of people, so too can even the most ordinary of thoughts. Thus, if the risk of frustrating others' desires doesn't generally affect the moral status of an action, then it generally won't affect the moral status of a thought either.

III

Yet even if most other people's desires have no bearing on the permissibility of our thoughts, there are some classes of individuals—most notably, romantic partners and close friends—whose desires may seem to have a special status. If a wife wants her husband not to fantasize about other women, then isn't each such fantasy a new betrayal? When one friend tells another about a recent triumph, shouldn't the other feel joy rather than indifference or resentment? Even if the husband's fantasies and the friend's indifference never come to light, hasn't each failed to satisfy a requirement that is rooted in the relationship itself?[6]

There is obviously something right about this. Relationships do impose requirements, and these may indeed include the requirements that husbands not fantasize obsessively about other women and that friends be pleased by one another's successes. It seems to me, though, that neither of these requirements, nor any other we might add, is best understood as a special case of a moral duty to bring one's private thoughts into conformity with a partner's desires. Instead, the better explanation of what is wrong with the friend's indifference and the husband's fantasies is that each belies the assumptions on which the relationship itself is founded.

For as Thomas Scanlon has convincingly written,[7] to be a party to a friendship (or, we may add, a familiar kind of romantic relationship), a person must (1) have a characteristic set of attitudes toward the other party and (2) believe that the other has similar attitudes toward him and (3) entertain various intentions, based on these shared attitudes, to do things with and for the other party. Where friendship is concerned, the attitudes that each party takes to be reciprocated include a desire to spend time with the other and a concern for his welfare, and the relevant intentions include plans to do things together and willingness to help when needed. Where one common form of romantic relationship is concerned, the attitudes that each party takes to be reciprocated include a desire to please and spend time with the other and to be his or her sole sexual partner, and the relevant intentions include plans to act on these

---

[6] Joseph Raz has argued that valuable relationships are defined precisely by the duties they involve; see his "Liberating Duties," *Law and Philosophy* 8 (1989), pp. 3–21.

[7] Thomas Scanlon, *Moral Dimensions* (Cambridge, MA: Harvard University Press, 2008), ch. 4.

desires. In each case, each party's intentions are conditional on the truth of his beliefs about the other party's attitudes and intentions.

But if this is so, then any private attitudes that *falsify* either party's beliefs about the other's attitudes, beliefs, or intentions must at the same time undermine the basis for any intentions that are based on them. Scanlon puts this point nicely when he writes:

> You are disposed to confide in a friend . . . because you suppose that the friend cares about you and how your life is going. Similarly, the particular kind of pleasure that you take in being with a friend presupposes that he or she takes pleasure in the interactions as well. If this is not so—if the other person is bored, or merely indulging you—then the whole thing is founded on a mistake.[8]

Without further information, we cannot tell whether the marriage and the friendship in our examples are similarly "founded in a mistake." However, even if they are not, the husband's fantasies and the friend's indifference remain unlikely to be a complete match with the beliefs and attitudes on which the relationship is founded.

For when the husband secretly indulges his sexual fantasies, he both falsifies any belief his wife may have about the exclusivity of his desire for her and frustrates whatever desire she has that that desire *be* exclusive. Thus, to whatever degree her intentions toward her husband are conditional upon either the truth of such a belief or the satisfaction of such a desire, those intentions must be ill-founded. Moreover, to whatever extent her intentions are constitutive of the relationship, their being ill-founded means that it too is ill-founded. These facts allow us to make sense of the claim that the husband has failed to satisfy the relationship's requirements without having to suppose that he has violated a moral duty; for if his fantasies imply that the relationship is defective, then any nondefective version of it must require their absence. On this account, the frustration of the wife's desire is indeed relevant to the husband's failure to satisfy the relationship's requirements, but what makes the desire's frustration relevant is not that his

---

[8] Ibid., p. 133.

frustrating it violates a moral duty that the relationship imposes, but rather that his doing so partially undermines the basis of the relationship itself. *Mutatis mutandis*, the same holds for the frustration of the woman's desire that her friend take pleasure in her success.

This argument relies heavily on a particular interpretation of the marriage and friendship in question, so it is natural to wonder whether the argument holds up when we alter that interpretation. However, when we try, we encounter an interesting asymmetry; for whereas a relationship in which one or both parties doesn't want or expect sexual exclusivity can still be a marriage, a relationship in which one or both parties doesn't care about the other is not really a friendship at all. Because the friendship relation doesn't appear to admit the kinds of variation that would put my argument to the test, we needn't consider it further but can proceed directly to marriage. Does my argument remain convincing when we suppose that the wife either (1) doesn't care if her husband wants other women or (2) would prefer that he didn't but is fully aware that he does?

At first glance, it may seem not to remain convincing; for if the wife either knows or doesn't care that her husband wants sex with other women, then the beliefs that support her intentions, and that therefore are partly constitutive of the relationship, will not include a belief that he wants sex with her alone. Because those constitutive beliefs will not be confounded by his fantasies, my account will no longer imply that his fantasies violate the relationship's requirements. However, the account's failure to support this implication will be problematic only if we still have the intuition that he *is* violating the relationship's requirements, and I, at least, do not. An open marriage may be unstable, but I can't see that either party is violating any of its requirements by seeking other partners. It's a bit more plausible to say that there's something unfair about a marriage that is built around a shared awareness that one party but not the other wants the other's desires to be exclusive, but even if this is so, what's unfair is not the violation of any requirement that is imposed *by* the relation but rather the internal structure of the relation itself. Because neither of these variants elicits the intuition that the husband's fantasies contravene the relationship's requirements, their introduction does not undermine, but if anything supports, the claim that what's problematic about the husband's fantasies in the original example is not that they're moral lapses, but rather that they signal trouble within the relationship itself.[9] One further objection warrants brief mention. My argument so far has been that we can make sense of the requirements that are violated by the husband's fantasies and the apparent friend's indifference without thinking of them as moral duties. However, to say this is not to rule out the possibility that the husband and the apparent friend are *also* violating moral duties. We plainly do owe things to our spouses and friends that we don't owe to others—help, deference, and emotional support, for example—and although the relation between these obligations and morality remains disputed,[10] there is no doubt that they are at least morality-like. However, if they are, then isn't the claim that we have a morality-like obligation to bring our private thoughts into conformity with our partners' desires a live option as well?

I do think this option remains formally alive, but I don't think we have much reason to accept it. What we owe to our spouses and friends is that we follow through on the intentions that are known to constitute our part of the relationship—intentions that are grounded in certain characteristic beliefs and attitudes about the other and that are directed at certain characteristic ways of interacting with him. Thus, if what we owed our spouses and friends included bringing our private thoughts into conformity with their desires, then an intention to do that would itself have to be among the intentions that constitute

[9] Can we say something similar about the negative thoughts that parents sometimes have about their children? Those thoughts may appear to pose problems for my account because the parent-child relation is both biological and asymmetric, and so need not involve the sorts of reciprocal beliefs and intentions on which relations like friendship and marriage are founded. It seems to me, though, if a child is really too young to care whether its parents resent or are embarrassed by it, then there's nothing wrong with their having these thoughts as long as they don't act on them, while if a child *is* old enough to care, then what's wrong with their negative thoughts is precisely that they belie the trust and sense of being loved on which the incipient relationship is founded. If these claims are correct, then the parent-child relation will be no more problematic than the others.

[10] For some relevant discussion, see Peter Railton, "Alienation, Consequentialism, and the Demands of Morality," *Philosophy and Public Affairs* 13, no. 2 (Spring 1984), pp. 134–71; Samuel Scheffler, "Relationships and Responsibilities," *Philosophy and Public Affairs* 13, no. 2 (Summer 1997), pp. 189–209; and Susan Wolf, "'One Thought Too Many': Love, Morality, and the Ordering of Commitment," in Ulrike Heuer and Gerald Lang, eds., *Luck, Value, and Commitment: Themes from the Ethics of Bernard Williams* (Oxford: Oxford University Press, 2012), pp. 71–92.

the relationship. However, this is implausible because tailoring one's thoughts to another's desires is *not* a way of interacting with him; it doesn't bring one into causal relation with him at all. In addition, and decisively, the private thoughts that are in question—caring for the other and wanting him or her alone as a sexual partner—are themselves among the ones that *ground* the relevant intentions, and so can hardly also be part of what is intended. Thus, we have little reason to suppose that their absence violates a morality-like obligation in addition to undermining the relationship itself.

IV

There is often little doubt about what our friends and intimates would like us to think, so in asking whether our relationships give rise to special duties to satisfy their desires, we have drifted away from the topic of moral risk. However, the second of our three routes from thought to harm—the one that involves the other's *discovery* of what we are thinking—brings us right back to risk. We are generally able to conceal our potentially hurtful thoughts, but we don't have total control over our facial expressions or our body language, and inadvertent slips are always possible. Thus, when we have such thoughts but try to keep them to ourselves, the likelihood that others will be hurt or offended is low but not negligible. Is the risk low enough to make the thoughts permissible?

As recent cultural trends amply demonstrate, people can take offense at just about anything. At the time of this writing, the activities that are publicly decried as offensive include enjoyment of ethnic food, jewelry, and styles ("cultural appropriation"), failures to use newly introduced pronouns (often involving repeated occurrences of the letters x and z), asking people where they're from, voicing unpopular political views, and, if she doesn't find you attractive, asking a woman for her phone number. In many of these cases—I would say all of them—it is tempting to dismiss those who take offense as unreasonable.[11] However, simply because each person is now widely believed to have

---

[11] Compare Mill: "[T]here is no parity between the feeling of a person for his own opinion and the feeling of another who is offended at his holding it, no more than

a right not to be offended, acting in these ways is often taken as an insult, and so is often accompanied by the sorts of resentment and pain that used to be reserved for intentional slurs and snubs. Because pain is pain no matter how it originates (and, of course, because the disclosure of some thoughts does legitimately cause it), the question of whether we are wrong to run the risk of having thoughts that would offend if they were discovered cannot simply be dismissed.

Here as earlier, the answer depends partly on whether inflicting the harm (in this case, the pain) is itself wrong and partly on whether the risk of inflicting it is too high to be defensible. As Scanlon has cogently argued, communicating a thought that another will find distressing is not always wrong. It isn't wrong, in particular, if the distressing thought expresses a justified moral criticism.[12] But most of the thoughts that bear on our current question are not like this; rather, some are intrinsically neutral beliefs and attitudes that persons with inflamed sensibilities find disturbing, while others are an unlovely stew whose ingredients include (in roughly ascending order of hurtfulness to most people) failures of empathy, ulterior motives, negative personal judgments, animosity and ill will, physical revulsion, dismissal based on group membership, and visceral racial or religious hatred. I'm not sure where on this spectrum of hurtful thoughts to draw the line between the ones that it is and isn't permissible to express, but I am convinced that there's a line to be drawn.[13] However, I'm also convinced that even when a thought would be maximally hurtful if it were expressed, the risk a person runs by merely thinking it is never high enough to make his doing so wrong.

My reason for saying this is not just that most of us are pretty good at maintaining neutral expressions and keeping our mouths shut, but also that even nonneutral facial expressions and body language are always

---

between the desire of a thief to take a purse and the desire of the right owner to keep it." John Stuart Mill, *On Liberty* (Indianapolis, IN: Bobbs-Merrill, 1956), p. 102.

[12] Thomas Scanlon, *What We Owe to Each Other* (Cambridge, MA: Harvard University Press, 1998), ch. 6, esp. pp. 282–90.

[13] This topic has been much discussed; for some representative readings, see Mari J. Matsuda, Charles R. Lawrence III, Richard Delgado, and Kimberle Williams Crenshaw, *Words That Wound: Critical Race Theory, Assaultive Speech, and the First Amendment* (Boulder, CO: Westview Press, 1993).

ambiguous. When a person remains silent but makes a sour face or displays signs of agitation, we often cannot be sure whether the cause is digestive upset, marital discord, lack of sleep, or something about our own words, actions, or presence. Moreover, even when we clearly *are* the occasion of his negative reaction, nothing short of a verbal explanation can make it clear what he is upset or angry or disgusted *about*. This is important because what determines whether any given thought is not at all troubling, mildly disturbing, or deeply hurtful is precisely its propositional content. What shocks and appalls is not our generalized awareness that the other doesn't like something about us, but rather our focused appreciation of his disdain for our intellect, irritation at our mannerisms, belief that we cut a ridiculous figure, indifference to our feelings or opinions, or deep disgust at the bare existence of people of our skin color or facial configuration. These are facts about what someone is thinking that his physical movements don't betray and that even the most involuntarily expressive among us can almost always blur.

Because only words can reveal the exact content of a person's thoughts, even a cursory attempt to conceal their content will inject considerable ambiguity into his behavior and appearance. In addition, even when others do get enough of the gist of one's thoughts to be upset by them, their upset is usually transient and does no lasting damage. For both reasons, the risk that our nasty thoughts will be transparent enough to cause serious distress does not seem great enough to support a prohibition against having them.[14]

---

[14] Here and elsewhere in this chapter, I am basing my argument on certain broad generalizations about human beings. This strategy seems inevitable in any discussion that turns on probabilities of harm, but it equally inevitably invites counterexamples. Can't we envision a situation in which another person will recognize exactly what we are thinking and be devastated by it? And can't we always construct cases in which the risk of thinking particular thoughts is unacceptably high by continuing to add zeros to the magnitudes of the harms that would ensue if others found out about them?

The answer, I think, is that such cases are indeed conceivable, but that this doesn't mean that any actual thoughts are too risky to think. In the real world, even those who know us best know only a small fraction of what we are thinking and feeling at any given time, and in the real world, too, the effects of leakage are rarely ruinous. These considerations suggest that from an ex ante perspective, the risks that attach to nasty thoughts are never prohibitively high. I am grateful to Michael McKenna and Steven Wall for pressing me to address this issue.

V

The third and final way in which private thoughts can cause harm—by motivating those who have them to act in harmful ways—is also the most serious. Anyone who has fantasies about shooting up a church or corrupting a child must see something attractive in these activities, and so must have at least some motivation to engage in them. Moreover, even if those who think in stereotyped or biased terms bear no ill will toward the objects of their bias, they must at least hold beliefs that in combination with many common desires (e.g., to hire the most qualified employee or keep the neighborhood safe) will provide them with motives to discriminate. In these and many other ways, the mere entertaining of a private thought can raise the likelihood that one will perform a public act that is both harmful and wrong.

Does this mean that entertaining the thought is itself wrong? According to Damian Cox and Michael Levine, the answer is often "yes." They characterize such thoughts as "moral hazards," defined as "situations and states that significantly enhance the likelihood of typical agents acting wrongly,"[15] and they write, "Moral judgment falls, not only on actions generated by a moral hazard, but on the hazard itself."[16] The thoughts they cite as examples of moral hazards include predatory sexual desires, beliefs that too closely track the evidence that close friends are guilty of serious crimes, and racist beliefs "that a preponderance of members of another race are sneaky, unintelligent, lazy, and hostile."[17] Although Cox and Levine grant that someone with strong moral convictions might have such thoughts but never act on them, they argue that this is in practice unlikely: "this fantasy of perfect moral self-governance is just that—a fantasy."[18] Because thought affects action in so many ways, there is no way to make sure that a bad thought will not break out into bad action. That is why it is wrong to have such thoughts in the first place.

---

[15] Damian Cox and Michael Levine, "Believing Badly," *Philosophical Papers* 33, no. 3 (November 2004), p. 216.
[16] Ibid., p. 217.
[17] Ibid., p. 219.
[18] Ibid.

As it stands, this argument is overstated. It cannot always be wrong to raise the likelihood that one will act wrongly in the future because even thoughts and actions that are manifestly innocent often do just that. Simply by attending a faculty meeting with my supremely irritating colleague, I raise the likelihood that I will snap and run amok; simply by driving to campus for the meeting, I raise the likelihood that I will accelerate through a yellow light and cause an accident; simply by holding the false belief that I am late, I further raise this likelihood. Despite these facts, it is not morally wrong for me to hold the false belief, to drive to campus, or to attend the meeting; and the reason in each case is that I am a normal person with a normal degree of self-control. My ability to control myself may not entirely eliminate the possibility that I will leap across the table at my colleague or cause a traffic accident, but it certainly reduces these risks to tolerable levels.

And, just so, the person who fantasizes about keeping a child chained in his basement but who understands that it is wrong to molest children (or is simply afraid of being caught) may have enough self-control to reduce nearly to zero the likelihood that he will act on his fantasy. Indeed, by providing him with a harmless release for his urges, his having the fantasy may actually *lower* the likelihood that he will actually molest a child. And, similarly, a person who secretly holds a certain group in contempt but is too principled or prudent to show it may be no more likely than anyone else to display overt bias or hostility. Because such self-control is the norm, the twisted fantasies and biased beliefs of those who acknowledge moral constraints on behavior do not often pose unacceptable risks of harmful action, and neither, *mutatis mutandis*, do any of their other nasty thoughts.

In saying this, I may appear to be overlooking the possibility of *hidden* bias, the unearthing of which has become a cottage industry. We obviously can't exercise control over a belief or tendency that we don't even know we have. However, precisely because they don't rise to the level of consciousness, our hidden biases are not among the mental events that constitute our private world. Thus, even if we are well aware that we are prejudiced at an unconscious level, our awareness of this cannot obligate us to avoid any of our conscious thoughts.

What may seem more likely to support such an obligation, though, is the possibility that our *conscious* biases might affect our behavior in ways of which we are not aware. Even when we are both conscious of having a particular bias and committed to not acting on it, we cannot rule out the possibility that it is skewing our attempts to do the right thing in ways of which we are *not* conscious.[19] If the resulting risk of wrongdoing is high enough, then won't *that* obligate us to eliminate the biased beliefs and attitudes of which we are conscious?

The answer, I think, is that although the unconscious effects of our conscious biases might indeed impede our efforts to do the right thing, they're no more likely to do so than the unconscious effects of many other kinds of conscious states. For all we know, our attempts to make fair decisions may also be distorted by the unconscious effects of our desires to advance our own projects or interests, our affection for our friends, our good or bad moods, or our feelings of comfort or discomfort in the presence of particular individuals. However, despite the notorious omnipresence of this possibility, the risk in the latter cases is not high enough to obligate us to do anything beyond trying our best to act fairly, and I see no reason to say anything different about the risk that is posed by bias.

Thus, as long as you, the reader, are someone who acknowledges the force of morality as it pertains to your public acts, it is unlikely that you will be led to act wrongly by your ugly thoughts and fantasies. You're in far more danger of being led astray by the everyday temptations of self-interest and laziness. For people like you, there is little risk in letting your mind run free.

VI

But what about those who are *not* like you? What of those who see no reason to do the right thing, who have radically misguided ideas of what morality demands, or who lack the strength of will to do what they should? When people like this have violent fantasies or hateful

---

[19] For discussion of one mechanism through which conscious thought can unconsciously affect behavior, see Susan Hurley, "Bypassing Conscious Control: Unconscious Imitation, Media Violence, and Freedom of Speech, in Susan Pockett, William P. Banks, and Shaun Gallagher, eds., *Does Consciousness Cause Behavior?* (Cambridge, MA: MIT Press, 2006), pp. 301–37.

thoughts, aren't they indeed rendered more likely to do something wrong? And doesn't this mean that they, at least, are obligated not to think those thoughts?

At least as concerns the first two types of case, I think the answer is a clear "no." In the case of the flat-out amoralist, the basic problem is that any moral requirement that he not think whatever thoughts would significantly raise his likelihood of his acting wrongly will simply be redundant. If someone cares so little about morality that he is willing to blow right past the requirement that he not gun down random members of the group that he so despises, then it's more than a little pointless to add the further requirement that he not even *think* of gunning any of them down. Where the amoralist is concerned, what needs adjusting is not our understanding of what morality requires, but rather his understanding of the force of its requirements.

The issue may seem different when we turn to what we might call the *twisted* moralist—that is, the person who is concerned to do the right thing but believes that killing infidels *is* right—since his not having that belief *would* reduce the chances of his acting wrongly. However, here again, there is more than a whiff of redundancy to the idea that morality might require the acceptance of its own requirements. The problem with this idea is not just that it raises the threat of an unchecked proliferation of moral requirements—i.e., of a need not only to augment the requirement that one not murder with a requirement that one accept the requirement that one not murder, but also to augment the latter requirement with a further requirement that one accept *it*, and so on without end. The deeper problem is that the reasons for believing that it is wrong to murder *just are* the reasons not to murder, and that if anyone fails to recognize the reasons not to murder, he will therefore also fail to recognize the reasons not to raise the risk of murdering by believing that murder is not wrong. Thus, here as earlier, postulating an additional moral requirement not to run the risk of having the relevant belief would simply be pointless.

The third type of case—that of the person who both knows what morality requires and cares about doing the right thing but lacks the will power to resist when attractive alternatives cross his mind—is the hardest for my account to accommodate. We all know what it is like to be tempted by the thought of a few (more) drinks, an unwise sexual adventure, or a clever but nasty retort, and while most of us have enough will power to retain control over our decisions, we also all know people who do not. For a person of the latter sort, the occurrence of the seductive thought is an inflection point; once it claims his attention, the odds that he will act wrongly go way up. When someone finds himself in this situation, isn't it indeed wrong for him to entertain the thought that poses the moral risk?[20]

There are, I think, arguments in both directions. The case for maintaining that it is *not* wrong for him to entertain the thought is grounded in a tension between the agential perspective and the external point of view that one must adopt in order to predict one's own moral lapses. When we approach the world as agents, we view ourselves as continuous with the versions of ourselves who will make decisions in the future, and to view oneself in this way is necessarily to view one's future options as genuinely open. This is, I think, the line of thought that leads Larry Alexander and Kimberley D. Kessler to write, "Defendant cannot view his own future choices as matters subject to his prediction.... [T]hose risks [of future misconduct] cannot materialize without a further choice or choices by defendant, a matter over which he believes himself to have total control."[21] As many philosophers (including, interestingly, both Hume and Kant) have noted, to approach the world as an agent is to be oblivious to whatever causal factors are influencing one's decision behind the scenes.[22] But if the agential perspective compels us to regard our future options as open, then how can even the weakest-willed of agents accept any prediction of backsliding that might imply that he is obligated to avoid a seductive thought?

---

[20] There are many who believe that morality's requirements extend only as far as our control. If someone accepts this view, then he will maintain that even if a thought does greatly raise the likelihood that someone will act wrongly, the person's having it is not wrong as long as it comes to him unbidden. In Chapter 1 I explicitly disavowed the idea that morality presupposes control, so this is not an argument I want to make, but to avoid needless distraction, I will in the remainder of the section consider only cases in which agents *are* able to avoid the thoughts or fantasies that tempt them to act wrongly.

[21] Larry Alexander and Kimberly D Kessler, "Mens Rea and Inchoate Crimes," *Journal of Criminal Law and Criminology* 87, no. 4 (1997), p. 1169.

[22] For Hume's version of this view, see David Hume, *Treatise of Human Nature*, ed. L. A. Selby-Bigge (Oxford: Oxford University Press, 1960), book II, part III, p. 408; for Kant's, see Immanuel Kant, *Groundwork of the Metaphysics of Morals*, trans. H. J. Paton (New York: Harper and Row, 1956), ch. 3, pp. 115–16.

That's the case for maintaining that weak-willed agents *cannot* be obligated to avoid the thoughts that significantly raise the likelihood of their acting wrongly. However, there's also a case in the other direction, and to appreciate it, we need only remind ourselves of the many contexts in which agents do rely on expectations about their future behavior to guide their current decisions. Some common examples are child molesters who stay away from school zones, paroled criminals who avoid their erstwhile associates, hot-tempered people who don't keep guns in the house, and alcoholics who decline the first of what they know would be many drinks. Because it clearly *is* possible to reconcile our sense of ourselves as continuous agents with predictions about how we will behave in the future, there appears to be a direct route from the premise that we are under a general obligation not to cause serious harm to others to the conclusion that we are under a secondary obligation to avoid whichever thoughts would sufficiently raise the likelihood of our doing so.[23]

Of these opposing arguments, the second may initially appear to be the stronger. However, to deploy that argument in support of the conclusion that certain thoughts are morally impermissible, one would need to back it with the supplementary premise that the risk that those thoughts will lead to wrong action is unacceptably high, and the countervailing argument may be read as calling this premise into question. It does so not by flatly denying that our past behavior can support expectations about what we will do in the future, but rather by implying that we always have the final say about whether those expectations will be met. Because we know that it will always remain up to us to decide whether to surrender yet again to whatever powerful temptation has overborne us in the past, we need not accept as authoritative any prediction about the likelihood of our doing so.[24] The indeterminacy that the agential perspective introduces into our assessment of the risk of future wrong action might not be significant if avoiding the risk had

[23] For an interesting defense of this view, see Eric A. Johnson, "Self-Mediated Risk in Criminal Law," *Law and Philosophy* 35 (2016), pp. 537–65.

[24] For contrasting views on the possibility of predicting one's own decisions, see Carl Ginet, "Can the Will Be Caused?," *Philosophical Review* 71, no. 1 (January 1962), pp. 49–55, and J. W. Roxbee Cox, "Can I Know Beforehand What I Am Going to Decide?," *Philosophical Review* 72, no. 1 (January 1963), pp. 88–92.

no major costs, since in that case the reasonable thing to do might be to play it safe.[25] However, in the chapters to come, I will argue that freedom of thought is among the great goods of human life, and that suppressing or avoiding any thought therefore does have a major cost. Although it's a close call, I'm inclined to take this to show that the risk of being led to act wrongly by even the most seductive of thoughts remains one that it is acceptable to run.

---

[25] For an argument against risking wrongdoing by killing beings of whose moral status we're uncertain, see Alexander A. Guerrero, "Don't Know, Don't Kill: Moral Ignorance, Culpability, and Caution," *Philosophical Studies* 136, no. 1 (August 25, 2007), pp. 59–97.

4

Vicious Thoughts

Early on, I conceded that the biased beliefs, malicious attitudes, and scurrilous fantasies can be vicious, but denied that this is equivalent to saying that such thoughts are morally wrong. But even if a thought's viciousness and its wrongness are not the same, it remains possible that its being vicious is enough to *make* it wrong, and many virtue theorists have said just this. To make their case, they appeal to a bridging principle that connects the badness of a vice to the wrongness of the acts and traits that manifest it. In the current chapter, I will critically discuss some prominent ways of elaborating that principle.

I

Although not all virtue theorists would accept the term, I will, for ease of exposition, refer to all versions of their bridging principle as definitions. Their general strategy in producing these definitions is to equate the right thing for an agent to do with whatever someone who was sufficiently virtuous *would* do in his situation, and to add that an act is wrong when it is one that a vicious but not a virtuous person would perform.[1] Because the virtues are widely thought to involve dispositions to feel, notice, and think as well as act, these definitions can easily be extended to apply to thoughts as well as acts; we can say, for example, that a thought is morally wrong when it is one that only a vicious person would have. On this account, the reason it is wrong to fantasize about torture, domination, and rape is that these are fantasies that no decent person would entertain.

---

[1] The most explicit and detailed formulation of these ideas appears in Rosalind Hursthouse, *On Virtue Ethics* (Oxford: Oxford University Press), 1999.

A Wild West of the Mind. George Sher, Oxford University Press (2021). © Oxford University Press.
DOI: 10.1093/oso/9780197564677.003.0004

As long as they are understood as mere stipulations, these definitions are unexceptionable, but a definition can contain the word "wrong" without capturing our standard conception of wrongness. We would hardly advance our understanding of morality if we used "wrong act" to mean "act performed while wearing a duck mask" or "thought that it is wrong to have" to mean "thought that occurs to one on a Tuesday." To invoke one of these definitions to contest my claim that no thoughts are morally wrong would simply be to change the subject. But are the virtue ethicists' definitions really any better?

This question is tricky because the nature of morality is itself controversial. Its essential features are sometimes, but not always, taken to include each of the following: prescriptivity or action-guidingness, a dominant or exclusive emphasis on the interpersonal, restriction to what agents can control, codifiability in terms of rules or principles, impartiality toward different people's interests, being universally binding, specifying what we owe to others, and being a source of reasons that preempt or override most if not all others. A number of these features are potentially relevant to the question of whether thoughts can be morally wrong, and I am inclined to agree that our standard conception of morality does include most (though not all) of them. However, the more of the contested features we take the standard conception of morality to include, the less compelling it will be to reject the virtue ethicist's definition on the grounds that it fails to capture the standard conception. For this reason, I will make no appeal to any of the cited features except the last. The only assumption I will make about our standard conception of morality is that the reasons it provides have a special force that others lack.

But am I really entitled to assume even this much? At first glance, I may seem not to be, for there is no shortage of theorists who believe that moral reasons do *not* have special force. Of these theorists, some believe that moral reasons do have force but are not overriding,[2] while others maintain that they have force only for those who already buy into morality.[3] However, while rejecting morality's special force is

---

[2] One philosopher who takes this position is Susan Wolf; see her "Moral Saints," *Journal of Philosophy* 79, no. 8 (August 1982), pp. 419–39.

[3] Proponents of views like this include Bernard Williams, "Internal and External Reasons," in his *Moral Luck: Philosophical Papers 1973–1980* (Cambridge: Cambridge

indeed a live option within metaethics, it is not an option that those who wish to extend morality's requirements into the private realm can afford to adopt; for if they did, they would have to acknowledge that whatever moral constraints on thought they favor are themselves without significant force. Thus, at least for dialectical purposes, it does seem safe to assume that moral reasons have some kind of special force.

That assumption is shared by many virtue ethicists,[4] and it provides a touchstone against which to evaluate their definition of wrongness as it pertains to thought. To qualify as adequate, that definition must allow us to understand, first, why the viciousness of a thought gives each person a reason not to think it and, second, why that reason is strong enough to preempt or override most if not all others. To provide answers to these questions, the virtue theorist must draw on some substantive account of what makes a trait a virtue or a vice in the first place. Thus, to get clear about the possibilities, we must begin with the notions of virtue and vice themselves.

II

Of the different accounts of virtue and vice that philosophers have proposed, some are clearly incapable of combining with the virtue ethicist's definitions of right and wrong. It would, for example, not be helpful to stipulate that what makes an act or thought morally wrong is that only a vicious person would perform or have it, but then to add that what makes someone vicious is that he is disposed to act and think

University Press, 1981), pp. 101–13, the early Philippa Foot, "Morality as a System of Hypothetical Imperatives," in her *Virtues and Vices* (Berkeley: University of California Press, 1978), pp. 157–73, and, more recently, Dale Dorsey, *The Limits of Moral Authority* (Oxford: Oxford University Press, 2016).

[4] "Moral reasons are special just because of this role they have in our deliberations: they override other kinds of reason just because of the kind of reason that they are. But now we have found similarity rather than difference with ancient virtue ethics. For all ancient theories think exactly the same way about the fact that the action is cowardly: this is a consideration which is not just weighed up against the profit and time expended, but which sweeps them aside; and to think otherwise is to misconstrue what cowardice is." Julia Annas, *The Morality of Happiness* (Oxford: Oxford University Press, 1993), pp. 121–22.

in ways that are morally wrong. That pairing would be both circular and uninformative: circular because it would define vice in terms of wrongness and wrongness in terms of vice, uninformative because we would have no way of breaking into the circle to find out either which acts and thoughts are wrong or which traits are vicious.

A bit less obviously, it also will not do to back the virtue ethicist's definition of wrongness with a mere enumeration of the traits that are to count as virtues and vices; for if we lack an understanding of what the entries on each list have in common, then we will have no way of understanding either why a trait's appearance on our list of virtues should give anyone a reason to have it or why its appearance on our list of vices should be a reason to avoid it. Things may improve a bit if we take our list of vices to be unified by the disapproval they elicit, since a trait's being disapproved of arguably does give us some reason to avoid instancing it. However, even if it does, any such reason will be weak and easily overridden, and so will lack the special force that is characteristic of moral reasons.

To avoid these difficulties, the virtue ethicist will have to back his definition of wrongness with an account of vice which explains why we have weighty reason to avoid it. Of the accounts that satisfy this requirement, the two most promising are eudaemonism and Platonism. According to the eudaemonist, a virtue is a trait that is conducive to its possessor's flourishing, while a vice is a trait that detracts from it; according to the Platonist, a virtue is a trait that is oriented toward the Good, while a vice is a trait that is either indifferent to the Good or actively oriented toward the Bad. Of these influential views, the first is promising because it offers the possibility of grounding our reasons to be virtuous in our weighty reason to pursue *our own* good, while the second is promising because it offers the possibility of grounding our reasons to be virtuous in our weighty reason to pursue *the* Good. If any account of virtue is to support the virtue ethicist's definition of wrongness, it is likely to be one or the other of these.

But I don't think either account does support that definition, and I now want to explain why. Because eudaemonism and Platonism raise very different issues, I will have to deal with them separately. I begin with eudaemonism.

III

To establish that each person has a morality-grade reason not to think certain thoughts, the eudaemonist must meet four challenges. First, he must demonstrate that each forbidden thought is suitably connected to some corresponding trait. Second, he must explain why each such trait detracts from its possessor's well-being in the way that gives him a weighty reason not to have it. Third, he must explain why a person's well-being gives him reason to avoid not only such traits but also the thoughts to which they give rise. And, fourth, he must explain why the person's reasons not to have the thoughts are not significantly less weighty than his reasons not to have the traits. If the eudaemonist fails to meet any one of these challenges, his explanation of why the targeted thoughts are morally wrong will not go through. In what follows, I will argue that he cannot fully meet any of them.

Before we can evaluate the claim that each forbidden thought is rooted in some corresponding trait, we must be specific about which thoughts we mean. Within the literature, the thoughts that are most often said to be morally off limits include (1) fantasies of rape, domination, and torture; (2) racial hatred and beliefs that some groups are inferior to others; and (3) malice and enjoyment of other people's suffering. Moreover, anyone who condemns any given thought in any of these categories will generally also condemn thoughts in all the others. Thus, fully to meet the first challenge, the eudaemonist will at a minimum have to establish that each thought in each category—henceforth, for brevity, each bad thought—is rooted in some corresponding bad trait.

But are bad thoughts really linked this closely to bad traits? Just as someone who is usually kind may on occasion lash out cruelly, can't someone who is deeply committed to racial equality occasionally be tickled by a scurrilous joke? And can't a genuinely benevolent person sometimes feel a pang of schadenfreude? If the answers to these questions are "yes," as they surely are, then our private reactions and feelings will not always match our broader traits. A bad thought's not being characteristic of a person does not mean that it is not rooted in his character, but it does mean that the thought is not a manifestation of a broad-gauged disposition to have similar thoughts under many disparate conditions. Hence, to preserve his claim that all bad thoughts are rooted in character, the eudaemonist will have to take the aspects of a person's character that connect him to what goes on in his mind to include even very narrow tendencies of thought.

But making this adjustment at the argument's first stage will bring complications at its second; for even if a full-fledged vice such as injustice or malice is seriously inimical to its possessor's well-being, it is far less plausible to say this about each narrow and rarely instanced disposition to behave or think badly. Given the immensely complicated interplay among each person's beliefs, attitudes, values, and other aspects of his psychology, there are bound to be indefinitely many bad things that each of us would do and think if the stars were lined up just right.[5] As long as these dispositions do not form a pattern, they seem too isolated and transient to be of much significance for our lives. But if these narrow dispositions can worsen our lives only minimally and only at the margins, then whatever self-interested reasons we have not to have them will not be weighty enough to sustain the eudaemonist's argument at its third and fourth stages.

If we can have a weighty reason to avoid a broad but not a narrow disposition to think a certain kind of thought, then the weightiness of that reason cannot be determined exclusively by what such thoughts are about. This means that the eudaemonist is not in a position to conclude that certain types of thought are morally off limits simply in virtue of their contents. Yet even if his argument implies only that certain *tokens* of certain types of thought are morally wrong, it will still threaten my claim that the subjective realm is morality-free. Thus, to assess the seriousness of that threat, we must now ask how well the eudaemonist can meet the remaining three challenges.

---

[5] For relevant discussion, see Stanley Milgram, *Obedience to Authority* (New York: Harper and Row, 1974); John Doris, *Lack of Character* (Cambridge: Cambridge University Press, 2002); and George Sher, *In Praise of Blame* (Oxford: Oxford University Press, 2006).

III

The second challenge, it will be recalled, is to explain why even a *broad* disposition to think bad thoughts should significantly worsen a person's life. The task of assessing the eudaemonist's ability to meet this challenge is complicated by the bewildering variety of things that have been said both about eudaemonia itself and about its relation to virtue. "Eudaemonia" is translated sometimes as "flourishing,"[6] sometimes as "happiness,"[7] and sometimes as "well-being."[8] Under each interpretation, its determinants are understood sometimes to consist of familiar goods such as enjoyment, success, and cooperative or gratifying relations with others,[9] but sometimes also of more exotic elements, including virtue itself.[10] Of those who take virtue to have some important connection to eudaemonia, some take the connection to be sufficiency,[11] others take it to be necessity,[12] and still others maintain only that the virtuous are more likely to achieve eudaemonia than others.[13] In each case, some take the connection to be epistemically accessible only to those who have already achieved a modicum of virtue,[14] while others take it to be accessible even to clear-thinking villains.[15]

Given this welter of cross-cutting views, the general question of whether having a vicious character worsens a person's life is not one

---

[6] John Cooper, *Reason and Human Good in Aristotle* (Cambridge, MA: Harvard University Press, 1975).

[7] Annas, *The Morality of Happiness.*

[8] L. W. Sumner, "Is Virtue Its Own Reward?," *Social Philosophy and Policy* 15, no. 1 (Winter 1998), pp. 18–36.

[9] See Philippa Foot, "Moral Beliefs," in her *Virtues and* Vices (Berkeley: University of California Press, 1978), Peter Singer, *How Are We to Live?* (Oxford: Oxford University Press, 1997), and Hursthouse, *On Virtue Ethics*, ch. 8.

[10] See John McDowell, "The Role of Eudaemonia in Aristotle's Ethics," in Amelie Rorty, ed., *Essays on Aristotle's Ethics* (Berkeley: University of California Press, 1980), pp. 359–76, and D. Z. Phillips, "Does It Pay to Be Good?," *Proceedings of the Aristotelian Society* 64 (1964–65), pp. 45–60.

[11] See John McDowell, "Virtue and Reason," in Roger Crisp and Michael Slote, eds., *Virtue Ethics* (Oxford: Oxford University Press, 1997), pp. 141–62. See also Annas, *The Morality of Happiness*, for the role of this thesis in ancient Stoic thought.

[12] Aristotle, *Nicomachean Ethics*, trans. Terence Irwin (Indianapolis, IN: Hackett, 1985).

[13] See Hursthouse, *On Virtue Ethics*, ch. 8.

[14] See Phillips, "Does It Pay to Be Good?" and McDowell, "Virtue and Reason."

[15] See Singer, "How Are We to Live?" and R. M. Hare, *Moral Thinking* (Oxford: Oxford University Press, 1981), ch. 11.

that can profitably be addressed here. However, it is worth noting that when eudaemonists answer the question in the affirmative, the vices they take as their central examples—injustice, dishonesty, cruelty, and the like—are oriented mainly to action. This raises the question of how much of what they say can be extended to broad dispositions whose instances are confined to bad thoughts. The answer, I think, is "not all that much."

For, first, as long as a person's bad thoughts do not influence his public behavior, there is little reason to expect the frequency with which he entertains them to affect either his ability to achieve his goals or the quality of his interactions or relationships with others. Because we run an additional risk of damaging our standing with others with each further lie we tell and each further unjust act we perform, a broad disposition to act in one of these ways is obviously more damaging than a narrow one, but nothing comparable is true of degraded fantasies, malicious pleasures, or prejudiced beliefs. The malign Walter Mitty incurs no external disadvantages, and neither, it seems, need he incur any that are internal. Malicious pleasures are, after all, still pleasures. We who are not malicious may not like them, but those who experience them often do, and the same holds for fantasies of domination, rape, and torture. More broadly, a person who inwardly gloats when he encounters discomfort or suffering, or whose worldview is organized around his abhorrence of the Zionist conspiracy or the evils of race mixing, may nevertheless live a normal, engaged life and may feel nothing but good about himself. By any standard measure, many who manage to keep their bad thoughts strictly to themselves are no worse off for being broadly disposed to have them.

Can the eudaemonist accommodate these observations by narrowing his thesis further? In addition to taking the dispositions to think bad thoughts that seriously worsen people's lives to be restricted to those that are broad rather than narrow, can he also take them to be restricted to some *subset* of the relevant broad dispositions? Can he say, in particular, that the dispositions to fantasize about domination and rape that seriously worsen a person's life (and so, if the rest of the argument goes through, are morally wrong) are only those that obsess him to the point of blocking out more constructive and enjoyable pursuits, cause him to feel self-disgust or self-loathing, or provide him with sufficiently urgent motivation to act in ways that will redound to his disadvantage? And, similarly, can the eudaemonist restrict the prejudices and hatreds that count as seriously worsening a person's life to those that will eventually burst forth in utterances or activities that elicit hostility or avoidance from others?

The answer, I think, is that he can indeed preserve a version of his argument by saying things like this, but that the cost of doing so will be to eliminate any remaining role that that argument might assign to the *contents* of the relevant thoughts. It is certainly true that some twisted fantasies are obsessive and paralyzing while others engender self-disgust and self-hatred, and that some biased beliefs lead people to do and say things that are seriously inimical to their interests. But it is no less true that a person who is obsessed about something innocent— the fortunes of the Houston Astros, say, or the decline of biodiversity or the scary mole on his arm—may also be blocked from constructive activities by his obsession and may also hate himself for it. Moreover, simple bad judgment is at least as likely to lead a person to do and say things that are seriously inimical to his interests as is any disposition to think bad thoughts. Because obsessive tendencies of thought can be just as harmful when the thoughts are virtuous as when they are vicious, the eudaemonist is hardly in a position to invoke their harmful effects to explain why only their vicious instances are morally wrong.

So far, I have considered only claims that broad dispositions to think bad thoughts are inimical to one or another familiar form of well-being. However, when eudaemonists maintain that vice makes us worse off, they sometimes understand the notion of worsening in a nonstandard way. They sometimes maintain, in particular, that the best conception of well-being is one that has virtue built right into it, and that the proper standpoint from which to understand this is precisely that of the virtuous agent himself. As Julia Annas puts the point, "Virtue . . . can transform a human life. It can do so because it can transform your view of what happiness is."[16] Along similar lines, Rosalind Hursthouse has written that to an honest person, "[t]he exercise of honesty (at least toward one's nearest and dearest and in pursuit

---

[16] Julia Annas, "Virtue and Eudaimonism," *Social Philosophy and Policy* 15, no. 1 (Winter 1998), p. 49.

of philosophy) is partially constitutive of what the speaker thinks of as flourishing or living well."[17] If the relation between vice and ill-being is similarly constitutive, and if broad dispositions to think bad thoughts are indeed vices, then every virtuous person will have good grounds to believe that we all have reason to avoid such dispositions.

But to the eudaemonist who wants to show that even those who are broadly disposed to think bad thoughts are *themselves* in possession of reasons not to have such dispositions, this implication is no help at all; for because the relevant conception of ill-being is by hypothesis not accessible from a standpoint external to that of the virtuous agent, an appeal to it cannot possibly convince those who do not occupy that standpoint. The problem is not merely that such an appeal cannot *motivate* a vicious person to change; it also does not appear to provide him with a *justification* for changing. The mere fact that he would accept the proposed conception if he became virtuous is no justification, since it is presumably no less true that the virtuous person would reject that conception if he became vicious. What is needed to resolve the impasse is some reason to believe that the former transformation would constitute progress while the latter would be a regression. However, such a reason, if it could be produced, would presumably favor virtue on some grounds other than its relation to well-being. Also, of course, any such reason would have to be provided from precisely the sort of external or neutral standpoint that the current proposal aspires to avoid.

IV

So far, I have argued that as long as the closet racist and the malign Walter Mitty are able to keep their bad thoughts strictly to themselves, there is little reason to believe that either would be better off without his broad disposition to think those thoughts. But suppose, next, that I am wrong about this. Suppose self-interest, understood in some expansive way, *does* give each of them a weighty reason not to have the relevant broad disposition. How, exactly, might that show that such

[17] Hursthouse, *On Virtue Ethics*, p. 169.

persons also have weighty reasons not to have bad thoughts on particular occasions?

This question—the third of our four challenges—may at first seem easy to answer; for because dispositions are manifested one instance at a time, it may seem obvious that anyone who has a strong reason to rid himself of a vicious disposition will have a reason of comparable strength to avoid each of its instances. However, on closer inspection, this is a non sequitur because avoiding a particular instance of a vice need not go any distance toward eliminating the vice itself. To be a cruel person is to have a deep and pervasive set of interlocking dispositions to enjoy the suffering of others, notice opportunities to inflict it, act on them when they arise, and fantasize about making people suffer, and these dispositions are unlikely to be much affected by the suppression of any given cruel thought.[18] Because the cruel person who suppresses the cruel thought remains cruel, his reasons not to have the vice will not by themselves be reasons not to have the thought, and the claim that he should not have the vice will not by itself imply that he *should* suppress the thought. It's true that he shouldn't be the kind of person who is *disposed* to have such thoughts, but given that he *is* that kind of person, his actually having them is neither here nor there.

This of course is not the end of the story. Inspired by Aristotle, many philosophers believe that the way to rid oneself of a vice is resolutely to resist the inclinations to which it gives rise over an extended period of time. If this view is correct, then someone who has a reason not to have a vice will indeed have a reason not to manifest it on any given occasion. However, even if this recipe for self-improvement is defensible— something about which I have my doubts—the contribution that any single refusal to think a cruel thought can make to the eradication of the corresponding vice will be minuscule at best. Because that contribution will be tiny, any resulting gains in eudaemonia will presumably be tiny as well. However, on the account we are considering, a person's reasons to be virtuous are supplied precisely by the eudaemonia that

---

[18] According to many, dispositions are not freestanding but are grounded in underlying physical or psychological states. If someone's broad disposition to think bad thoughts is grounded in this way, then the persistence of the grounding state will be a further factor that is unaffected by his avoidance of the disposition's potential instances.

he will thereby gain, and this suggests that when the expected gains are small, the reasons will be correspondingly weak.[19] Thus, all in all, it is implausible to expect a person's reason to resist any particular instance of a vice to be nearly as weighty as his reason to rid himself of the whole thing.

But if so, then the eudaemonist's attempt to explain why vicious thoughts are wrong will collapse; for as we have seen, explaining this would mean establishing not only that each person has some reason to avoid each ugly fantasy, biased belief, and cruel thought, but also that each such reason is weighty enough to dominate or preempt nearly all others. Reasons grounded in marginal gains in eudaemonia seem far too weak to have this effect. Thus, even if the eudaemonist can meet our third challenge by taking a person's weighty reason not to be broadly disposed to think a given kind of bad thought to be distributed over all of that disposition's potential instances, the cost of his doing so would be to weaken each of the distributed reasons in a way that prevents it from meeting our fourth and final challenge.

V

Quite apart from its inability to establish that anyone has a morality-grade reason not to indulge in retrograde fantasies or gloat about a rival's agonizing illness, the eudaemonist's approach to these matters has the wrong structure. Although I have not rested my own argument on this claim, I agree with those who argue that our reasons to

---

[19] It's not always true that a person's reason to perform an action that will get him one-nth of the way to a goal is only one-nth as strong as his reason for seeking that goal. His reason for performing the action will be stronger if his doing so now is causally necessary for performing similar actions later (as when he won't be motivated to stay on his diet tomorrow unless he stays on it today), or if in its absence all the other actions in the sequence won't get him to the goal (as when he won't be able to make his car payment without saving a certain amount every single day). His reason to perform the act will also be stronger if performing it means doing his part in a cooperative scheme in which n–1 other people are also doing theirs. But attempts to gain eudaemonia by avoiding vicious thoughts don't appear to conform to any such pattern, and so the strength of one's reason to make any such attempt does seem proportional to the amount of eudaemonia it can be expected to yield. I owe my appreciation of the need to address this issue to Daniel Pallies.

seek our own well-being are too self-centered to be the basis for our moral obligations to others. In this regard, the Platonistic view, which asserts that a virtue is a trait that is somehow oriented to the Good, has a definite advantage; for although the idea of the Good can be filled out in many ways, it is obviously broad enough to encompass the well-being of others. In addition, as the Platonistic approach is elaborated by contemporaries such as Robert Merrihew Adams and Thomas Hurka,[20] it explicitly counts thoughts as well as actions as virtuous or vicious.

For when Hurka elaborates his claim that virtue is loving the good and hating the bad, he does so by characterizing loving x as "desiring, pursuing, or taking pleasure in x"[21] and by offering corresponding characterizations of hating. Of these ways of loving something, desiring it and taking pleasure in it can both be done privately. And, similarly, when Adams identifies moral virtue with "persisting excellence in being for the good,"[22] he takes the ways of being for something to include "loving it, liking it, respecting it, wanting it, wishing for it, appreciating it, [and] thinking highly of it."[23] These again are all states that occur mainly if not exclusively within the private realm.

Can this Platonistic understanding of vice support the conclusion that at least some vicious thoughts are morally off limits? At first glance, the question here may seem to be only whether the badness of thoughts that involve a love of the bad is a source of reasons not to have them that are recognizably moral. However, although I do think this question may in the end be central, I also think there is a prior question that needs to be addressed first. Put most simply, the prior question is whether a thought's satisfying the recursive definition of vice (the phrase is Hurka's) gives us *any reason at all* to avoid having it.

---

[20] See Robert Merrihew Adams, *A Theory of Virtue* (Oxford: Oxford University Press, 2006) and Thomas Hurka, *Virtue, Vice, and Value* (New York: Oxford University Press, 2000). In classifying these philosophers as Platonists, I don't mean to imply that they accept any particular metaphysical view, let along Plato's own. Instead, I mean to say only that each takes goodness to have some sort of objective existence and takes virtue to consist of one or another positive stance toward it. For a further account that is not explicitly concerned with virtue but otherwise has the same structure, see Robert Nozick, *Philosophical Explanations* (Cambridge, MA: Harvard University Press, 1981), ch. 5.
[21] Ibid., p. 15.
[22] Adams, *A Theory of Virtue*, p. 14.
[23] Ibid., pp. 15–16.

The reason this question requires independent attention is that there is a clear distinction between the analytical claim that vice consists of being for the bad or against the good and the normative claim that an attitude's being a vice in this sense makes it bad in a way that gives us reason not to have it. Despite the strong associative connection between vice and badness, the analytical claim does not entail the normative one, and the normative claim seems far more plausible when being for the bad involves actively promoting it than when it involves only privately liking or being pleased by it. To establish that we have reason not to be entertained by the newspaper's police blotter or be amused by scurrilous or disgusting jokes, one would need a substantive argument that went well beyond an appeal to the elegance of the recursive definition. However, as far as I can see, no convincing argument of this sort has yet been produced.[24]

Is the assumption that we have reason not to be for the bad plausible on its face? I am honestly not sure. On the one hand, I think any sophisticated inventory of what is good and interesting about human subjectivity will have to include many ways of flirting with the bad, and that these flirtations are badly distorted when we describe them simply as being *for* the bad. However, on the other, it does seem to me that some private attitudes toward the bad—fantasizing about detonating nail-filled bombs in crowded malls and taking delight in others' agonizing illnesses may serve as examples—are indeed bad in a sense that gives us reason to avoid them. Because I see no principled way of organizing the terrain, I am torn among the views that (1) we have at least some reason to avoid every thought that involves a positive attitude toward the bad, that (2) although some such thoughts are extremely ugly and repulsive, we never have any reason to avoid them, and that (3) there is

---

[24] In *Philosophical Explanations*, Nozick locates a thing's disvalue in a kind of disunity among its elements, and locates the badness of valuing what is disvaluable in a higher-order form of that same kind of disunity. This proposal, if successful, would in effect be a defense of the recursive approach. However, as I have argued elsewhere, Nozick's aestheticized criterion of value makes it hard to see why a thing's value should make it something that is worth wanting and seeking. In addition, as Hurka has suggested, Nozick's conception of unity appears to differ in its lower-order and higher-order uses: "In the base-clauses of Nozick's theory, 'unity' means one thing, correspondence to something real, whereas in the recursion-clauses it means another, a positive orientation toward what need not be real" (*Virtue, Vice, and Value*, p. 39).

indeed a principle that explains why we have reason to avoid some but not all of them, but it has not yet been brought to light.

But which of these options we choose does not matter much, since even if we grant that *all* of the thoughts that satisfy the recursive definition of vice are bad in a sense that gives us reason not to have them, those reasons will again fall short of supporting the claim that having such thoughts is wrong. Whatever else is true, it is surely far worse to promote or seek the bad than simply to take private pleasure in its existence. As Adams sensibly writes:

> Why do we condemn *Schadenfreude* less severely than ruthlessness without malice? The obvious answer is that *Schadenfreude*, even where it is a settled vice, does not necessarily involve any willingness to contribute causally to the evils in which it finds delight. Being for or against goods in thought or feeling deserves less weight in the overall evaluation of character if it remains passive, involving no tendency or will to show itself in ethically important action or inaction. One who is not disposed to contribute causally to the realization of an evil, if that were possible, is less strongly for it. [25]

Because our reasons not to harbor private affection for what is bad are evidently quite weak, they do not seem capable of preempting or dominating others in the way that moral reasons are thought to do. At best, they may tip the balance against our having vicious thoughts when they are not defeated by such further considerations as the pleasure those thoughts would bring.

Of course, if those who accept the recursive definition of vice are consequentialists about the right, as Hurka in fact is,[26] then they can respond to this objection by pointing out that the mere possibility of tipping the balance in this way is itself sufficient to show that vicious thoughts can be wrong as well as bad. However, to retreat to this position would again be to relinquish the ambition of establishing that

---

[25] Adams, *A Theory of Virtue*, p. 44.
[26] On this point Hurka and Adams part company, for instead of embracing consequentialism, Adams construes moral obligations as requirements that are imposed by valuable relationships. Because he understands morality in this way, Adams regards vicious thoughts as bad but not wrong.

certain kinds of thoughts are always wrong simply in virtue of their content. The combination of consequentialism and the recursive account is incapable of capturing this intuition because it must hold that even the most vicious of thoughts are permissible as long as the benefits they bring are great enough. Because this view's judgments of wrongness are always hostage to contingency, they lack the absoluteness on which the moralist insists. In addition, although I am not yet in a position to make the case, I will argue in a later chapter that even the nastiest of private thoughts are inseparable from the free play of the intellect that is itself among life's greatest goods—an argument that, if correct, will suggest that a vicious thought's badness never does tip the consequentialist balance in a way that makes having it wrong.

VI

Virtue ethicists generally understand virtues and vices as dispositions to think, feel, and notice as well as act, but I think it is fair to say that most give pride of place to what the virtuous person would *do*. There is, however, a variant of the approach, influentially developed by Iris Murdoch, which places its main emphasis not on public action but on the private reflection that precedes it. According to Murdoch, our public choices have their origins in the many private acts of attention that collectively shape the way we *see* the situations within which we must choose and act. This means that "at crucial moments of choice most of the business of choosing is already over."[27] Because Murdoch takes the important work of morality to be done internally and privately, and also because she holds that a just and loving attention to the particular can reveal aspects of a transcendent good, her approach may appear to offer an alternative route from a Platonism-infused account of virtue to the conclusion that the private realm is subject to moral regulation.

I doubt that Murdoch herself would want to follow this path; for she expresses disdain both for philosophical approaches whose normative

---

[27] Iris Murdoch, *The Sovereignty of Good* (New York: Schocken, 1971), p. 37.

vocabulary is confined to schematic terms such as "good" and "right" and for the related tendency to take all the important normative questions to concern right action.[28] Because she holds these views, her insistence on the importance of the inner life seems unlikely to yield a direct or unequivocal answer to the question of whether thoughts can be morally wrong. Still, because her views do have implications about how we should think, we may reasonably wonder how close they bring us to the kinds of moral constraints that we are discussing.

I will turn to that question shortly, but before I do, I want to summarize the aspects of Murdoch's account that seem most relevant to it. Writing in the 1950s and 1960s, Murdoch defined her position in opposition to what she regarded as a widely held view of agency incorporating elements of behaviorism, existentialism, and utilitarianism. This unlikely trio was said to share a view of the self as a simple center of will, devoid of value commitments, and a corresponding view of choice as a lurch toward an arbitrarily preferred member of a set of prepackaged alternatives. On this account, to deliberate is simply to draw on neutral factual information to establish which of the available alternatives will best satisfy one's own (or perhaps other people's) ungrounded preferences.

But Murdoch argues that this picture misses something essential. In actuality, our options are *not* prepackaged, and the central moral task is precisely to discern the proper vocabulary in which to formulate them. Murdoch illustrates both the importance and the subtlety of this task in her celebrated example of a mother-in-law, M, and her daughter-in-law, D. In that example, M's initial impression is that D is "not exactly common yet certainly unpolished and lacking in dignity and refinement. D is inclined to be pert and familiar, insufficiently ceremonious, brusque, sometimes positively rude, always tiresomely juvenile."[29] However, aware that her own motives and attitudes may

---

[28] Along these lines, she writes deploringly that "the idea of goodness (and of virtue) has been largely superseded in Western moral philosophy by the idea of rightness, supported perhaps by some conception of sincerity" (ibid., p. 53), and she adds, "I think it is more than a verbal point that what should be aimed at is goodness, and not freedom or right action, although right action, and freedom in the sense of humility, are the natural products of appeals to the Good" (ibid., p. 71).

[29] Ibid., p. 17.

be distorting her vision, M considers D sympathetically and carefully, and in consequence comes to see more. Under the new dispensation, D emerges as "not vulgar but refreshingly simple, not undignified but spontaneous, not noisy but gay, not tiresomely juvenile but delightfully youthful, and so on."[30]

This example encapsulates many of Murdoch's leading ideas, of which the following four seem most pertinent to our concerns. First, as Murdoch makes clear, M's reevaluation of D is not just a shift but an improvement: "Some people might say 'she deludes herself' while others would say she was moved by love or justice. I am picturing a case where I would find the latter description appropriate."[31] Second, M's reevaluation is virtuous because it *is* motivated by love and justice. To attempt to see others lovingly and justly is to respond to the pull of an ideal of the good that is at once elusive and inescapable: "Good is the magnetic center toward which love naturally moves."[32] Third, the central impediment to achieving a just and loving vision is the needy and demanding self and the tissue of fantasy that it constructs to protect itself from a reality that it cannot bear to confront: "In the moral life the enemy is the fat relentless ego."[33] And, fourth, although in the actual example M's revised understanding of D has no impact on her actions, it is easy to imagine circumstances in which it could and should: "If we picture the agent as compelled by obedience to the reality he can see . . . he will be saying 'This is A B C D' (normative-descriptive words) and action will follow naturally."[34]

As should be obvious, any serious examination of this collection of ideas would lead us into a thicket of vexing metaphysical, epistemological, and normative questions. To avoid entanglement (or at least to stay out of the thicket's densest areas), I won't question Murdoch's basic assumptions but instead will confine my attention to what they imply about how we should think.

---

[30] Ibid., pp. 17–18.
[31] Ibid., p. 18.
[32] Ibid., p. 102.
[33] Ibid., p. 52.
[34] Ibid., p. 42.

VII

There are, I think, two lines of argument to consider: first, that we should strive for a just and loving appreciation of others because without this we cannot know how we should act toward them and, second, that we should do so because such an understanding is worth having just in itself. These arguments are of course not mutually exclusive, and I suspect that Murdoch would take them somehow to merge,[35] but from our perspective they are worth considering separately.

The first argument draws some credibility from a pair of truisms: first, that we generally cannot know what we should do without knowing the relevant features of our situation and, second, that facts about other individuals are generally central elements *of* our situation. There is, to be sure, an apparent tension in the idea that our appreciation of those individuals must be at once just and loving, since an accurate appreciation, which is presumably required by justice, may well include awareness of features that are decidedly unlovable. However, to resolve this tension, it may be sufficient to maintain that the awareness must be both as penetrating as possible and as sympathetic as is consistent with what that degree of penetration discloses. Assuming that this (or some other) way of resolving the tension will work, the question we must now ask is whether the premise that paying just and loving attention to others is often a prerequisite for knowing how we should act can support anything resembling a moral requirement on thought.

The answer, I think, is that this is unlikely; for the contexts in which just and loving attention appears most necessary for knowing what one

---

[35] That Murdoch wishes to connect the two lines of thought is strongly suggested by the striking fact that she adumbrates both within the space of a single page. The first emerges clearly when she writes that "true vision occasions right conduct. . . . The more the separateness and differentness of other people is realized, and the fact seen that another man has needs and wishes as demanding as one's own, the harder it becomes to treat that person as a thing" (ibid., p. 66). By contrast, the second claim is implicit in her contention, in the very next paragraph, that the artist, who often is not thinking of anyone in particular, is also subject to the demands of truth and love: "The great artist sees his objects (and this is true whether they are sad, absurd, repulsive, or even evil) in a light of justice and mercy. The direction of attention is, contrary to nature, outward, away from self which reduces all to a false unity, toward the great surprising variety of the world, and the ability so to direct attention is love" (ibid.).

should do are precisely the ones in which our failure to act as we should looks least like a moral failure. On the one hand, we don't need to know much about a person in order to keep our word to him, treat him fairly, refrain from coercing him, or spare him pain, so fulfilling these familiar sorts of moral obligations does *not* appear to require that we know the other in any deep way. On the other hand, we sometimes *do* need to know a lot about a person in order to know (say) whether criticism or praise would do him more good or how to advise him about an important choice; but this also doesn't appear to support a moral obligation to attend to him justly or lovingly because we are generally not morally *obligated* to provide others with constructive criticism or advice. This is not to say that we never have such obligations, but it is to say that the obligations, when they exist, are rooted in our particular relationships to particular individuals. When someone cannot fulfill an obligation of this sort without paying just and loving attention to another, there is indeed a sense in which his paying such attention is required. However, as I argued in the previous chapter, what this comes to is only that if he does not attend justly and lovingly to the other, then an expectation that is internal to the relationship will be violated, and so the relationship will to that extent be defective. Thus, here again, there does not appear to be any *moral* requirement whose satisfaction requires a just or loving vision of the other.

This is hardly a knock-down argument. For one thing, the boundaries of morality are too elastic to support a confident rejection of the claim that we can be morally obligated to pay just and loving attention to our friends and intimates. In addition, as Murdoch often stresses, the potential objects of our just and loving attention are not restricted to particular other individuals. For example, when our situation is complicated, we may need to think hard about it to disentangle and prioritize the relevant factors, while when selfishness tempts us, the effort of imagining the reality of others may serve to counteract its effects. Murdoch in effect illustrates both phenomena when she asks:

> Should a retarded child be kept at home or sent to an institution? Should an elderly relative who is a trouble-maker be cared for or asked to go away? Should an unhappy marriage be continued for the

sake of the children? Should I leave my family in order to do political work? Should I neglect them in order to practice my art? The love which brings the right answer is an exercise of justice and realism in really *looking*.[36]

Might the fact that morally right action can require *these* forms of careful attention give rise to a distinct moral obligation to make the requisite mental effort?

Once again, I think the answer is "no," for even if we grant both that it is morally wrong to institutionalize the retarded child and that the agent will come to realize this only if he thinks hard about his decision and its impact on the child and perhaps others, it remains implausible to understand his not thinking hard as a further and independent wrong. There is, for one thing, a puzzle about when the alleged wrong is supposed to occur, since at each moment before he acts the agent may permissibly put off thinking hard until later, while once the action is performed there *is* no later and so the only thing left to be wrongful is the act itself. In addition, to invoke an act's wrongness to establish the wrongness of the agent's prior failure to reflect, one would need to argue either that (1) when the action is performed, its wrongness flows back to the agent's failure, or that (2) at some point (which?) before he acted, the unreflective agent created an unacceptable risk that he *would* subsequently act wrongly. I argued against the first strategy in Chapter 2 and against the second in Chapter 3, and in light of these arguments, it seems much cleaner to restrict our moral condemnation to the single act of institutionalizing the child. If the agent's lack of careful thought enters at all, it does so only as part of the description of the act that merits our opprobrium.

The other way of invoking Murdoch's views in support of a moral obligation to reflect justly and lovingly—to argue that clarity of vision is worth having just in itself—is at once more appealing and more problematic. It's more appealing because a deep and accurate vision of things is obviously (at least to philosophers) very desirable, while

---

[36] Ibid., p. 91; emphasis in original.

it's more problematic because the gap between the goodness of such a vision and the wrongness of not seeking or achieving it is equally obvious. However good it is to see things accurately and fully, do we do something wrong if we try but fail or fail to try? Isn't the proper reaction to muddled thinking pity rather than condemnation?

If these questions are to have answers, the reasoning behind them will have to draw on the substance of Murdoch's metaphysical and normative views. Because I have resolved to avoid discussion of those views, I won't pursue the questions further, but instead will end with two brief general observations.

First, although any successful demonstration that we are morally obligated to seek a just and loving vision of others would indeed falsify my thesis that nothing in the private realm is morally off limits, it would not, by itself, make contact with any of the specific beliefs or attitudes or fantasies to which moralists about the mental object most strenuously. Although Murdoch would no doubt insist that fantasies about dominating others are pathologies of the omnivorous ego and that really looking at someone is incompatible with believing that he is inferior to others, any defense of these claims would have to be grounded in a substantive theory of psychodynamics and a substantive account of what really looking involves. The obvious danger is that these grounding premises will be tailored to the desired moral conclusions rather than freestanding.

Moreover, second, I think there is independent reason to doubt that any sane conception of morality is going to condemn anyone for not attempting the combination of hyperfocused attention and mysticism-tinged openness to experience that Murdoch found so appealing. We're not all novelists, and it makes no more sense to require that someone with a coarse sensibility and a limited attention span aspire to a refined understanding of others than it would to require that someone with a withered leg aspire to complete the triathlon. A deep and accurate understanding of reality may represent the pinnacle of human achievement, but many can't even get to the foothills. We learn from Kant that everyone must be able to do what morality commands, and we learn from the rule-utilitarians that this requires easily graspable rules. To achieve the universality that it needs to govern the lives of the mediocre and unimaginative as well as the discerning and subtle, a moral code must meet both desiderata. This doesn't mean that such a code can't prohibit certain kinds of thoughts—that's a substantive claim for which I am trying to provide a substantive defense—but it does mean that its requirements must be a lot more user-friendly than "really look."

5

Don't Even Think of It

Claims that rape fantasies, malicious attitudes, and biased beliefs are wrong just in themselves have a strongly deontological flavor, but contemporary deontologists have had strikingly little to say in their defense. The lone exception is Angela Smith, who has sought to derive constraints on thought from Thomas Scanlon's influential version of contractualism. In the current chapter, I will begin by critically examining Smith's arguments. Then, because other contemporaries have largely ignored the issue, I will turn directly to Kant's own theory, the locus classicus of deontological thought, and will ask whether his theoretical apparatus might enable us to justify certain constraints on thought. Although I am under no illusions about my ability to get to the bottom of Kant's theory—it's something you can get lost in forever—my tentative conclusion will be that no convincing deontological argument for putting any thoughts off limits is yet in sight.

I

According to Scanlon, our commitment to morality is rooted in the aim of interacting with others in ways that we can justify to them, and that aim is satisfied whenever our actions conform to principles that no one who shares it can reasonably reject.[1] If we understand morality in this way, then whether its requirements extend to purely private thoughts will depend on whether there *are* any restrictions on thought that no one could reasonably reject. Although Scanlon himself does

---

[1] The canonical statement of this view appears in Thomas Scanlon, *What We Owe to Each Other* (Cambridge, MA: Harvard University Press, 1998).

A Wild West of the Mind. George Sher, Oxford University Press (2021). © Oxford University Press.
DOI: 10.1093/oso/9780197564677.003.0005

not address this question,[2] Angela Smith has done so on his behalf, and in her view, the answer is a clear "yes."

Despite her sympathy with the moralistic position, Smith is careful to dissociate herself from the more extreme forms that restrictions on thought might take. She concedes, for example, that we can reasonably reject a principle that requires us *never* to have negative attitudes toward others, for "[i]f someone treats me or other people with moral disrespect or indifference . . . it seems perfectly appropriate to respond to such moral wrongs with negative attitudes of disapproval, resentment, or indignation."[3] She concedes, as well, that we can reasonably reject a principle "requiring that we have attitudes of love and deep concern for all others,"[4] for such a principle would impose demands that greatly outrun our emotional resources. However, Smith sees no comparable objection to a principle "requiring us to have basic attitudes of respect and goodwill toward others"[5]—one that forbids private feelings of contempt based on race, sex, or sexual orientation, rules out even covertly demeaning and belittling attitudes, and requires compassion toward those who suffer and indignation at violations of moral status. Because this principle locates the recognition that we owe to others in our attitudes toward them as well as our treatment of them, Smith dubs it "the Attitudinal Recognition Principle."

Why, exactly, does Smith think no one can reasonably reject the Attitudinal Recognition Principle? The answer, she writes, is that

> knowing that others did not accept that the relation of mutual recognition required the presence of certain attitudes would significantly affect the sort of moral relationship I could aspire to have with them. I could not take it for granted, for example, that they would

---

[2] The closest he comes is his suggestion, on page 175 of *What We Owe to Each Other*, that some sexual fantasies might involve attitudes that "are incompatible with what we owe to others." However, Scanlon does not pursue this suggestion.

[3] Angela Smith, "Guilty Thoughts," in Carla Bagnoli, ed., *Morality and the Emotions* (Oxford: Oxford University Press, 2011), p. 253.

[4] Ibid.

[5] Ibid.

not wish ill upon me or regard me with contempt, even if I knew that they would behave in morally permissible ways in their interaction with me.[6]

Thus, in Smith's view, what makes it reasonable to accept a principle requiring internal goodwill toward others is the aim of achieving a deep form of moral fellowship with them: "for those of us who aspire to stand in [such a relation] . . . there are strong reasons to insist upon the Attitudinal Recognition Principle over the Behavioral Recognition Principle."[7]

Does this reasoning yield a convincing defense of the Attitudinal Recognition Principle? The answer, I think, is that it does not, but that where it goes wrong depends on how tight a relation Smith takes to obtain between wanting to interact with others on mutually acceptable terms and aspiring to deep moral fellowship with them. On the one hand, if she merely takes there to be a substantial overlap, as her cagy "for those of us who aspire" formulation suggests, then the challenge to her position will be that some of those who wish to interact on mutually acceptable terms *without* aspiring to deep fellowship seem likely to find the suppression of their private ill will to be so burdensome as to give them reason to reject any principle that requires it. As long as any such individuals exist, the Attitudinal Recognition Principle will be one that some who wish to interact on mutually acceptable terms *can* reasonably reject, and so it will fail the Scanlonian test. On the other hand, if Smith takes the connection between wanting to interact with others on mutually acceptable terms and seeking deep fellowship with them to be internal or necessary—if she maintains that aspiring to deep fellowship *is part of what is involved* in wanting to interact on mutually acceptable terms—then the challenge will be to defend the proposed internal connection in a way that goes beyond mere stipulation. Let me now elaborate each challenge with an eye to explaining why I think neither can be met.

---

[6] Ibid., p. 254.
[7] Ibid., pp. 254–55.

II

Consider first the possibility that there can be individuals who want to interact with others on mutually acceptable terms *without* aspiring to any form of deep moral fellowship. If someone like this is to have reason to accept a principle that forbids even private ill will, it will have to be because he wants others not to bear private ill will toward him. However, in fact, people appear to vary widely in how much they care about others' private attitudes. At least offhand, it seems that most of us manage to live quite comfortably with the knowledge that many others privately regard us or our kind with antipathy and disdain, and that those others would be quite unmoved by an awareness of our suffering. I, for one, would be quite happy to live in a world in which some undetermined but very large number of people felt hostility and contempt toward people like me (as in fact I do) as long as they all were scrupulous about publicly conforming to principles that no one can reasonably reject (as in fact they are not). As long as strangers treat me right, I don't need their goodwill (although of course I'm happy to have it). For friendship, I look to my friends.

Moreover, just as people vary widely in how much they care about whether others privately wish them well, so too do they vary widely in how burdensome they would find it to suppress all of their *own* contemptuous, biased, and malicious thoughts. There are, I suspect, many to whom this would be burdensome indeed; for any conscientious person who was committed to a principle that required that he think only good thoughts would be locked in an endless battle with the weeds of envy, malice, and worse that kept invading his mental garden. That battle would be draining and frustrating: it's hard enough to get rid of a simple earworm, let alone to suppress a whole panoply of unacceptable thoughts. Moreover, the more conscientious the person was, the more debilitating he would find the guilt that attached to his innumerable unavoidable failures. A person's willingness to put up with these hardships can be expected to vary with both his individual psychology and his circumstances, but there are bound to be many to whom they would be enough of a burden to make it reasonable to reject the principle that imposes them.

III

So if Smith is to establish that no one who seeks to interact with others on mutually acceptable terms can reject a principle that prohibits hostile and malicious private thoughts, it will have to be on the alternative grounds that a commitment to deep fellowship is *built right into* the aim of interacting on mutually acceptable terms. Her claim will have to be that only those who have such a commitment can genuinely entertain the aim of acting only on principles that no one can reasonably reject. If this claim can be sustained, then it will not be surprising if the nonrejectable principles do turn out to require the suppression of private ill will; for such ill will, if allowed to persist, will undermine the very aim from which the principles themselves derive their authority.

But why, exactly, should we suppose that the aim of interacting with others on terms that no one can reasonably reject can only be rooted in an aspiration to achieve a form of fellowship that is this deep? We may certainly concede that *one* way to arrive at this aim is to ground it in this form of deep fellowship, but the crucial question is not how deep a relationship *can* be to give rise to the aim, but rather how deep a relationship *must* be to give rise to it. Moreover, as far as I can see, neither Smith nor Scanlon has offered us any reason to believe that there cannot be people who are quite comfortable with their own pockets of private contempt and malice, yet who also find it important not to interact with others in ways that cannot be justified to them. This combination of attitudes, indeed, appears to be more the rule than the exception.

Of those whose aim of interacting with others on mutually acceptable terms is not backed by goodwill toward all, some can be expected to have that aim for the standard Kantian reason that we owe this form of respect to all rational self-lawgivers, while others are apt to base it on different facts about their fellows—on their ability to hold other agents to account or reflect on their own motives, for example, or on each person's existence as an independent center of subjectivity whose own aims matter just as much to him as ours do to us. Of these various ways of justifying the aim (which are of course not mutually exclusive), none requires either an actual attitude of goodwill toward all or an aspiration to acquire such an attitude. Hence, in each case, the principles to which the aim gives rise will be able to allow private ill will without undercutting the basis for their authority.

Although these considerations do show that someone can entertain the aim of interacting with others on mutually acceptable terms without accepting a principle that requires private goodwill, they may not quite seem to establish that anyone can entertain that aim without accepting *some* restrictions on his private thoughts; for whatever facts a person takes to underwrite the aim, there remains one class of thoughts that does seem capable of undercutting it, namely, any thoughts that imply that these facts do *not* really support the aim. For a Kantian, for example, the subversive thoughts will include doubts that other people really are rational self-lawgivers, doubts about whether rational self-lawgivers are really owed respect, and doubts about whether respecting them requires acting only on principles that can be justified to them. Alternatively, if someone thinks it important to justify himself to others because he views their interests as no less important than his own, then for him the subversive thought will be that the interests of others are *not* really this important. Also, of course, for those who seek to interact with others on mutually acceptable terms because they aspire to a form of deep fellowship that requires mutual goodwill, the subversive thought will be that this form of deep fellowship is not really worth having.

Because this objection pegs its restrictions on each person's private thoughts to the reasoning that prevents *that person* from treating others in ways that he cannot justify to them, it falls short of establishing that there is any single kind of private thought that no one is allowed to have. In addition, it affords little purchase on the kinds of private thoughts and attitudes that moralistically inclined philosophers are standardly inclined to condemn: it doesn't tell us much about what is wrong with torture fantasies, private racial bias, or schadenfreude. Thus, even if the objection did compel some retreat from the bald claim that the private realm is morality-free, it would leave us with plenty of room to accept a trimmed-down version of that claim.

But, properly understood, the objection doesn't compel any retreat at all; for if a person were to reject the belief that undergirds his aim of acting only in ways that he can justify to others, then precisely in so doing he would also deprive that aim of the authority that it needs to provide him with a reason to *retain* the belief. Whatever is wrong with regicide, its wrongness cannot reside in its violation of a king's sovereignty because the moment the act is consummated is precisely the moment that king ceases to *be* sovereign. And, just so, whatever might be wrong with a Scanlonian's coming to believe that deep fellowship is not really worth having, the problem cannot lie in his new belief's incompatibility with his aim of interacting with others on mutually acceptable terms; for the moment he acquires the new belief is precisely the moment at which that aim loses its authority for him.

IV

Although Scanlon is not a Kantian, his contractualism is clearly in the Kantian tradition. Thus, by arguing that Scanlon's theory does not allow us to justify constraints on thought, we have already made some headway toward establishing that the dominant deontological approach will not support them. But what, next, of the connections between those constraints and Kant's own theory?

Kant himself is not shy about extending the demands of morality into the private realm. He is, for example, clearly saying that we have a duty not to entertain sexual fantasies when he writes that "lust is called unnatural if a man is aroused to it not by a real object but by his imagining it. . . . That such an unnatural use (and so misuse) of one's sexual attribute is a violation of duty *to oneself*, and indeed one contrary to morality in its highest degree, occurs to everyone immediately, with the thought of it."[8] He also seems to have duties of thought in mind when he writes that "while it is not in itself a duty to share the sufferings (as well as the joys) of others, it is a duty to sympathize actively in their fate,"[9] and that "in these vices [of envy, ingratitude, and malice] . . . hatred is not open and violent but secret and veiled, adding meanness to one's neglect of duty to one's neighbor, so that one also

---

[8] Immanuel Kant, *The Metaphysics of Morals*, trans. Mary Gregor (Cambridge: Cambridge University Press, 1991), pp. 220–21; emphasis in original.
[9] Ibid., p. 250.

violates a duty to oneself."[10] To what extent do these claims draw support from Kant's justificatory apparatus?

Kant's central doctrines and the relations among them have been interpreted in many ways, and any serious attempt to engage with this body of scholarship would exceed both our scope and my competence. Thus, instead of trying to do that, I will simply ask what the most important of those doctrines imply about the moral status of thoughts when we take them at something like face value. The doctrines on which I will focus are Kant's universalizability test, the idea that each rational being is an end in himself, the idea that all rational agency commands our respect, and the idea that we all have duties of self-perfection. Although each doctrine is potentially relevant to the question of whether morality governs our private thoughts, I will argue that each is far better suited to support duties of public action than duties of private thought.

Where the universalizability test is concerned, the first thing to notice is that many of the thoughts that moralists condemn most eagerly involve no mental agency at all. No one chooses to be disgusted by gay sex or to feel a secret thrill when a plane goes down; when these reactions come, they come unbidden. The involuntary nature of these thoughts is significant because the universalizability test applies to people's maxims, and these are defined as the subjective principles that encapsulate their reasons for acting. Because unchosen feelings and attitudes aren't mental actions, they can't be mental actions that are performed for reasons, and so they can't be associated with maxims at all.[11] This means that there simply isn't anything whose nonuniversalizability could *establish* the impermissibility of such a feeling or attitude. Because so much of what goes on in our minds is not subject to conscious control, the thoughts to which the

---

[10] Ibid., p. 251.

[11] Kant acknowledges this in several places, among them the passage in which he writes, about our duty to love others, "In this context, however, love is not to be understood as *feeling*, that is, as pleasure in the perfection of other men; love is not to be understood as *delight* in them (since others cannot put one under an obligation to have feelings). It must rather be thought of as the maxim of *benevolence* (practical love), which results in beneficence" (ibid., p. 244). For relevant discussion, see Marcia Baron, *Kantian Ethics Almost without Apology* (Ithaca, NY: Cornell University Press, 1995), ch. 6.

universalizability test applies are at best a small fraction of those that moralists condemn.

Moreover, of the relatively few thoughts that agents do choose to have, it is hard to see how any could *fail* the universalizability test. A person's maxim is nonuniversalizable if a world in which everyone acted on it either could not be described without contradiction or else would frustrate some future aim that the person will or might have. However, it seems quite possible to will the universal adoption of a maxim such as "Fantasize freely about sexual violence" or "Privately indulge your hatred of Jews" without arriving at a contradiction of either conception or will. It is not incoherent to suppose that everyone might secretly fantasize about violence or hate Jews (Jews certainly can hate themselves), so a world in which everyone harbors such thoughts can easily be conceived. Moreover, as long as the shared fantasies and hatreds did not break out into public action, it is hard to see how their omnipresence could frustrate any actual or possible practical aims. Thus, unlike the deceptive promises, neglected talents, and failures to render aid that famously fail the universalizability test, whatever vicious thoughts a person can keep strictly to himself will apparently pass it with flying colors.

Can those thoughts also pass Kant's second test, which requires that we not treat anyone merely as a means? This question is harder to answer because what is involved in treating someone merely as a means is not entirely clear. Kant clearly holds that we violate this requirement whenever we deceive, defraud, coerce, or otherwise treat others in ways to which they do not or cannot agree, but because these activities all involve causal interaction, it is unclear whether the phenomenon they illustrate can also be present when a person's thoughts do *not* causally affect others.

It would, I think, be hard to stretch the idea of treating someone merely as a means far enough to cover feelings such as schadenfreude, attitudes such as contempt, or beliefs about racial inferiority; for because we typically don't entertain these feelings, attitudes, and beliefs with any aim in mind, there is usually nothing for the person we are thinking about to be a means *to*. But other private states, such as fantasies of torture and sexual domination, often are entertained for a purpose. When someone courts such a fantasy, he typically does so because he expects to find it gratifying, and the courtship is typically conducted without the consent of the person fantasized about. When people discover that they have played a starring role in another's sick fantasy, they often react with horror and disgust. Because the fantasist seeks gratification by assigning another a role in his fantasy to which the other has not consented, his doing so may look like a textbook case of treating that other merely as a means.

But this can't be the whole story, since if we did treat someone merely as a means whenever we sought pleasure by thinking about him without his consent, then violations of the injunction not to do so would be omnipresent. We would then be violating the injunction not only when we fantasized about torture or sexual violence but also whenever we replayed an interesting conversation in our minds, thought fondly of an absent friend, or took pleasure in anticipating a social occasion. Needless to say, there is nothing wrong with doing any of this. Thus, if fantasizing about torture or sexual domination is wrong *because* it treats others merely as means, then treating someone merely as a means must involve some further wrong-making element.

Two candidates immediately suggest themselves. First, it may be proposed that whereas the absent friend who hasn't consented to be thought about fondly *would* consent if asked, the object of a torture fantasy not only hasn't consented but wouldn't. On this account, consent remains crucial, but the relevant form of it is hypothetical rather than actual. Alternatively, it may be suggested that what distinguishes memories of interesting conversations from fantasies about torture or sexual domination is that interesting conversations are themselves morally permissible while torture and sexual domination are not. On this account, what matters is not whether a thought or fantasy would elicit any form of consent, but rather the moral status of what it is about.

Might either proposal explain why fantasies about torture and sexual domination are wrong while fond thoughts and pleasant memories are not? Once again, I have my doubts. The problem with locating the difference in the fact that fond memories but not torture fantasies would be consented to is familiar: it is that what people would agree to depends too much on their individual psychology to support the kind of principled distinction that the moralist seeks. On the one hand, there are many who would be quite unfazed by the idea that others are having a grand old time fantasizing about hurting or humiliating them. (My own response, if I were asked for permission with the assurance that the fantasy would never leak out into the public realm, would be "Go ahead, knock yourself out.") And, going the other way, we can also easily imagine why someone might *not* consent to another's remembering a shared conversation or thinking of him fondly: perhaps he finds his part of the conversation embarrassing, or perhaps the other's fondness is not reciprocated. Because counterfactuals about consent are so variable, no account that relies on them will allow us to draw a clear boundary between permissible and impermissible thoughts.

The other suggestion—that the reason torture fantasies violate the injunction against treating others merely as means is that torture is itself wrong—is not vulnerable to this objection. If torture is wrong at all, then it will remain wrong no matter who does it or thinks about doing it to whom, and so all fantasies about it will fall on the same side of the line. Moreover, under the test for wrongness now under consideration, what makes it wrong to torture someone is precisely that doing so treats him merely as a means to some further end.[12] Thus, the broader principle that underlies the current suggestion is that whether an unconsented-to thought treats someone as a mere means depends on whether it is a fantasy about doing something that would *itself* count as treating him as a mere means.

This principle has a certain elegance, in that it takes one and the same feature of an act—its treating someone as a mere means—to imply both that the act is wrong and that gaining pleasure from thinking about it is wrong. However, precisely because of this, we may wonder how any feature of an act could affect the moral status of anything as different from it as a thought. As Christopher Cherry notes, the view that an act's wrongness extends to fantasies about performing it will not be convincing if "the differences between maleficent fantasy and actual evil-doing are simply *declared* morally irrelevant or insignificant, and a world of 'inner' harms and damages which duplicates the world of

---

[12] For subtle discussion of the ways in which torture differs from the many other activities that treat persons merely as means, see David Sussman, "What's Wrong with Torture?," *Philosophy and Public Affairs* 33, no. 1 (January 2005), pp. 1–33.

realities is simply posited."[13] Thus, the challenge to those who favor the proposed interpretation of Kant's second test is to explain *why* what makes it wrong to treat someone as a mere means should also make it wrong to fantasize privately about doing so.

V

To assess this challenge, let us look more closely at the difference between treating people as ends and treating them merely as means. As many have noted, there is more to treating someone merely as a means than simply furthering our own aims through our interactions with him. We further our own aims whenever we buy food from a grocery clerk, send a query to a journal editor, or ask someone how to get to the interstate, but as long as we do not coerce or deceive the other, he retains the option of withholding his cooperation. Thus, if he chooses to give it, there is a sense in which he gives it freely. By contrast, when we do coerce or deceive someone, we bypass his rational agency by depriving him of the opportunity to decide for himself whether to cooperate, and so we use him as we would a tool. However, according to Kant, it is precisely the capacity for rational agency that makes each person irreplaceably valuable, and hence an end in himself.[14] This allows him to say that coercing and deceiving (and a fortiori torturing and raping) fail to respect the very capacity that gives each person a value that is beyond any price.

Might an extension of this reasoning also explain what's wrong with *fantasizing* about torture or rape? Might it be argued, in particular, that just as rapists and torturers fail to respect their victims' own capacity for agency, so too do those who are merely willing to entertain the *thought* of acting in these ways? And, if so, then won't Kant indeed be able to offer a unified explanation of why vicious acts and fantasies about them are both wrong?

[13] Christopher Cherry, "When Is Fantasizing Morally Bad?," *Philosophical Investigations* 11, no. 2 (April 1988), p. 116.
[14] For an especially illuminating discussion of these ideas, see Christine Korsgaard, "Kant's Formula of Humanity," in her *Creating the Kingdom of Ends* (Cambridge: Cambridge University Press, 1996), pp. 106–32.

It is hard to deny either that fantasies about torture and rape are profoundly disrespectful to rational agents or that treating people as ends in themselves *requires* respecting their rational agency. However, even together, these claims will only yield a unified explanation of why torturing and fantasizing about it are wrong if they both use "respect" in the same sense, and on inspection, I don't think they do. It is one thing to respect a person's rational agency in the sense of not interfering with its exercise, and quite another to respect it in the sense of regarding it as uniquely valuable or as having a worth beyond all price. Respecting in the first sense is something we do in the public world, while respect in the second sense is an attitude that we have internally. The two senses may be connected to the extent that preventing someone from exercising his rational agency also displays a disrespectful attitude toward him, but the converse entailment clearly does not hold. It is quite possible to fail to respect another's autonomy in the second, attitudinal sense (for example, by fantasizing about torturing him) while strictly respecting his autonomy in the first, behavioral sense. Thus, to complete the argument, Kant would have to show that treatment as an end requires attitudinal as well as behavioral respect for rational agency.

Kant takes our moral duties to be imposed by our own practical reason. Thus, to establish that we have a duty to maintain a respectful attitude toward the rational agency of others, he must explain why having such an attitude is among the requirements of practical reason. But precisely because practical reason *is* practical, it is unclear how this is to be done. Within Kant's moral psychology, there is a sharp separation between motives of inclination, which are supplied by desires, impulses, and other states that we merely find ourselves having, and the often opposing motives of practical reason that we actively embrace. Moreover, when a person is seized with an impulse to steal or murder, what Kant takes practical reason to require is not that he not have that impulse, but only that he resist the inclination to act on it. (Indeed, there are notorious passages in which Kant seems to suggest that a right action does not have moral worth unless the agent does have to overcome some countervailing inclination.) Thus, by parallel reasoning, shouldn't Kant take practical reason to require not that we never *have* disrespectful attitudes toward others, but only that we never allow them to affect what we do? As long as our disrespectful attitude doesn't influence our public behavior, why, from the standpoint of practical reason, should our merely having it be any more wrong than our being seized with impulses of anger or greed?

As long as the duty to maintain a respectful attitude is understood as one that we owe to others, this question will be hard to answer. However, it is worth noting that Kant often characterizes duties of thought as ones that we owe *to ourselves*. This characterization is significant because it suggests that we may be looking in the wrong place when we ask why disrespectful attitudes are wrong. The real problem with such an attitude, it may be said, is that it violates its possessor's duty "to carry the cultivation of his *will* up to the purest virtuous disposition, in which the *law* becomes also the incentive to his actions that conform with duty and he obeys the law from duty."[15] On this account, what's wrong with fantasizing about torture or sexual domination (and, we may add, with countenancing private malice, envy, contempt, or bias) is that thinking in these ways diminishes or fails to promote the moral perfection that our *own* practical agency enjoins us to pursue. By neglecting this duty, we wrong not others but ourselves.

If our disrespectful attitudes toward others detract from our own moral perfection, then when practical reason enjoins us to seek such perfection, it must indeed require that we try to rid ourselves of them. In this way, the shift in focus from duties to others to duties to ourselves represents a genuine advance in the discussion. However, the proposed rationale for ridding ourselves of our disrespectful attitudes is only as strong as its premise that those attitudes do detract from our moral perfection, and it is hard to see how this can be true unless those attitudes are either wrong in themselves or conducive to other wrongdoing. Because their wrongness is precisely what is at issue, we will not advance the discussion by helping ourselves to it; we would move in a circle if we were to argue that fantasies about rape and torture are wrong because they display disrespect for others' rational agency, that displaying such disrespect is wrong because it violates our duty to seek our own moral perfection, and that fantasies about

---

[15] Ibid., pp. 191–92; emphases in original.

rape and torture detract from our moral perfection because having them is wrong. It would not similarly beg the question to argue that such fantasies detract from our moral perfection by raising the likelihood that we will *act* wrongly, but anyone who argued this way would simply be mounting a variant of the moral hazard argument whose shortcomings were discussed at length in Chapter 3. Thus, in either case, the strategy of grounding constraints on thought in the moral duty of self-improvement seems no less problematic than the other strategies we have examined.

VI

My argument to this point has been relentlessly negative. To defend my claim that the subjective realm is morality-free, I have marched (a bit mechanically) through the three major theoretical approaches to normative ethics and have argued that none compels us to maintain that morality constrains our private beliefs, attitudes, or fantasies. This way of approaching the issues is appropriate to my thesis, but it leaves quite a few loose ends. To bring these into the open, and so to bring out the need for a supplementary argument of a different and more positive sort, it will be helpful to review the main kinds of question that have been left unresolved.

An initial question is simply whether there are other, better ways of defending moral constraints on thought that I have not addressed. The current chapter leaves unexplored an indefinite range of further arguments that a resourceful Kantian might advance, and the same can obviously be said about arguments that might be devised by resourceful consequentialists and virtue ethicists (to say nothing of pluralists, particularists, and theorists of other stripes). There is, therefore, an obvious problem about closure.

Second, some of what I have said is admittedly speculative and/or controversial. For example, I acknowledged at the end of Chapter 3 that it is unclear whether our continuing ability to falsify predictions of our own wrongdoing can make it morally acceptable for us to entertain the kinds of thoughts that have led us to act wrongly in the past. In that chapter, too, I advanced a deflationary view of what is wrong with treacherous thoughts about spouses and friends that some are likely to find uncongenial. In addition, there is clearly room for further discussion both of what I say about Kant, Murdoch, and other figures and of the various empirical, philosophical, and normative assumptions on which I rely. So in these ways, too, my arguments are less than complete.

And, third, it is possible to construct particular cases in which general moral principles intuitively do appear to obligate us to think in certain ways. It may seem, for example, that someone could incur an obligation not to think about a romantic incident in his past by promising his wife that he won't. Alternatively, a scientist may be obligated not to work out a weapons design problem in his head if he knows that his evil captors will torture the secret out of him. The ingenious reader will no doubt be able to construct further examples along these lines.

Taken together, these unresolved issues exert a good deal of pressure on my brash assertion that the subjective realm is morality-free. If they cannot be disarmed, then I will have to retreat to the more modest claim that the constraints that morality imposes on thought are far less sweeping than many have thought. This would still be worth saying, but it would be far less interesting than the original bolder thesis. But such a retreat will not be called for if my piecemeal negative arguments can be backed by a sufficiently powerful and general positive argument for regarding the subjective realm as morality-free. I believe, in fact, that such an argument is available, and the book's remaining chapters will be devoted to its elaboration and defense.

6

Like Dye in Water

The positive case for excluding moral considerations from the subjective realm turns on the surpassing value of mental freedom. To make that case, I will have to argue, first, that the self-imposed constraints of morality would diminish our mental freedom to a greater extent than has yet been appreciated and, second, that the resulting lack of freedom would do more damage to our *lives* than has yet been appreciated. Of these claims, the first will be defended in the current chapter and the second in a concluding Chapter 7. Although both claims were anticipated in Chapter 1, it will turn out that there is much more to say about each.

I

Most of what goes on within our minds is not freely chosen. We don't choose to love or hate the people we do, and neither do we choose to be amused by tasteless jokes, feel secret thrills when the high are brought low, or drift into titillating fantasies. We also don't exercise much control over what we believe; although some philosophers do regard beliefs as voluntary enough to support attributions of responsibility,[1] doxastic voluntarism is implausible on its face. But if we don't freely choose our beliefs, attitudes, or fantasies in the first place, then how can a morality that purports to govern those thoughts pose any *threat* to our mental freedom?

---

[1] See, for example, Nishi Shah, "Clearing Space for Doxastic Voluntarism," *The Monist* 85, no. 3 (2002), pp. 436–45; Sharon Ryan, "Doxastic Compatibilism and the Ethics of Belief," *Philosophical Studies* 114 (2003), pp. 47–79; and A. K. Floweree, "Agency of Belief and Intention," *Synthese* 194, no. 8 (2017), pp. 2763–84.

A Wild West of the Mind. George Sher, Oxford University Press (2021). © Oxford University Press.
DOI: 10.1093/oso/9780197564677.003.0006

I think this question can be answered in more than one way, but before I can explain why, I will have to make two distinctions, one between two kinds of process that can lead to thoughts over which we lack direct control, and another between two kinds of freedom that are compatible with our lack of direct control over these thoughts. Because the two distinctions cut across each other, they enable us to specify four distinct ways in which our freedom can be threatened by prohibitions against thoughts over which we lack direct control. Strictly speaking, these threats are posed not by the prohibitions themselves but rather by what happens when we accept them. However, the fact that our acceptance threatens our freedom remains an objection to the prohibitions themselves because a morality can fulfill its function of governing our behavior only if we *do* accept the prohibitions it imposes.

My first distinction, between the two kinds of process that can lead to thoughts over which we lack direct control, turns on the role of reason in producing those thoughts. Of the thoughts that moralists condemn, some come about exclusively or mainly as a result of association or other nonrational processes, while others are partially or entirely dependent on evidence and logic. The clearest members of the first class are the thoughts we have while woolgathering, daydreaming, or fantasizing; for these are determined mainly by the patterns of association that are rooted in our history and secondarily by our particular desires and preoccupations in concert with the natural bent of our character. Our attitudes toward other people (for example, disdain, malice, superiority, and their opposites) are more mixed; on the one hand, they are informed by pictures of the world that are partly evidence-based, but on the other, they are differentiated by patterns of affect and desire whose genesis is nonrational. A fortiori, the same can be said of the emotional reactions through which our attitudes find expression on particular occasions.

However, and in clear contrast, what a person believes generally *is* determined primarily by (what he takes to be) his reasons. Although our beliefs are of course subject to many nonrational influences, the central pillar of their existence is our evidence for them. There are puzzles aplenty about how beliefs gain evidential support—about the justificatory role of sensory experience, memory, testimony, logic, and much else—but what we see as our epistemic reasons clearly play a central causal role in determining what we believe. When we believe that the price of gas is rising, that the accused is innocent, or that hydrogen is an element, we standardly do so because we either hold other beliefs that we take to support the relevant proposition or else have held such beliefs at some point in the past.[2]

The other distinction I want to make, between two ways in which thoughts over which we lack direct control can be free, mirrors a long-standing disagreement about the relation between freedom and choice. According to one tradition, represented by bare-bones compatibilists such as Hobbes and Ayer, freedom is simply the absence of impediments.[3] On this account, whether an unimpeded action or abstention is freely chosen in any deeper sense is neither here nor there. By contrast, another tradition, represented both by libertarians and by many other compatibilists, insists that an absence of impediments is at best a necessary condition for freedom, and that a further necessary condition is that one's actions or abstentions be related to one's choices in the right sort of way.[4] Of these competing conceptions of freedom, each captures something valuable about the notion, and each offers us a way of understanding how even a thought over which we lack direct control can display a form of freedom that would be threatened by an internalized moral prohibition.

For suppose, first, that we do take choice to be necessary for freedom. Put most simply, the reason this conception of freedom can apply to thoughts over which we lack direct control is that what we *choose* often extends beyond what we directly control. I am currently choosing to write the words that are appearing on my screen despite

---

[2] For defense of the view that we can remain justified in holding beliefs whose grounds we have forgotten, see Gilbert Harman, *Change in View* (Cambridge, MA: Bradford, 1986), ch. 4 and passim.

[3] See Thomas Hobbes, *Leviathan* (New York: Washington Square Press, 1964), ch. 14, and A. J. Ayer, "Freedom and Necessity," in Derk Pereboom, ed., *Free Will* (Indianapolis, IN: Hackett, 1977), pp. 110–18.

[4] For an incompatibilist version of this idea, see C. A. Campbell, "Is 'Freewill' a Pseudo-Problem?," in Bernard Berofsky, ed., *Free Will and Determinism* (New York: Harper and Row, 1966), pp. 112–35. For two compatibilist versions that differ radically in the way they conceive the role of choice, see R. E. Hobart, "Free Will as Involving Determinism and Inconceivable without It," in Berofsky, *Free Will and Determinism*, pp. 63–96, and John Fischer and Mark Ravizza, *Responsibility and Control* (Cambridge: Cambridge University Press, 1998).

the fact that I directly control only the contact that my fingers make with the keyboard, and I may similarly choose to avoid a thought over which I lack direct control by performing some other mental act that I expect will prevent it. I may, for example, be able to do this by intentionally turning my attention to another subject or aborting a line of inquiry that is trending in the forbidden direction. If I am able to perform some mental act that will enable me to avoid a thought that I am not allowed to have, then I am likely to be under a derivative obligation to do so. Thus, even when a given thought is not within my direct control, my commitment to a moral scheme that prohibits it may still reduce my mental freedom by limiting the choices I view myself as free to make.

There is, moreover, also a further way in which internalized prohibitions on thought can make us less free; for even if a given thought is entirely beyond the reach of choice, my conviction that having it would be wrong may still restrict my freedom by impeding what would otherwise be the natural flow of my ideas. Even if I entirely lack control over my impulses to gloat about others' misfortunes, my conviction that it is wrong to gloat may itself interact with other elements of my psychology in ways that either prevent me from gloating altogether or else alter its experiential character. My moral conviction may entirely prevent me from gloating if my aversion to guilt feelings is strong enough, and it will complicate the phenomenology of the gloating even if it is not that strong. *Mutatis mutandis*, the same will hold for my conviction that it is wrong to hold a certain belief; for that conviction is bound to affect the impact of any further beliefs that I would otherwise view as evidence for the forbidden belief. When our moral commitments do thus alter the flow of our thoughts, they reduce our freedom not in the way that threats and prison bars reduce the options among which agents can choose, but rather in the way that rocks and beaver dams disrupt the course of freely flowing rivers. Whether these reroutings are worsenings or improvements is of course a further question to which we will have to return.

As noted earlier, the two distinctions I have just made—between thoughts with nonrational and rational causes, and between undermining a person's mental freedom by narrowing his choice-options and by impeding the flow of his thought—cut across each other. Because they do, they enable us to distinguish four different ways in which an internalized constraint on thought can undermine a person's freedom. It can do so by

1. requiring him intentionally to disrupt a nonrational causal sequence that would otherwise lead to the forbidden thought; or
2. requiring him intentionally to abandon a line of investigation that would otherwise lead to the forbidden thought; or
3. causally disrupting a nonrational sequence that would otherwise lead to the forbidden thought; or
4. causally disrupting a rational sequence that would otherwise lead to the forbidden thought.

Although these threats to freedom are not all equally important, I will argue in the next chapter that each is far more serious than has generally been appreciated. However, before I can mount that argument, I will have to say a good deal more about how each threat works.

II

To bring out the structure of the first pair of threats, it will be helpful to begin with an example. Let us therefore suppose that in addition to forbidding me to shoot you, the moral scheme that I accept forbids me even to *think* of shooting you. Because I lack direct control over what occurs to me, I cannot obey the latter prohibition by simply choosing not to think of shooting you. However, I may at least be able to make it less likely that I will have the forbidden thought by exercising my mental agency in certain other ways. It may be, for example, that to guard against thinking of shooting you, I must turn my attention away from the many wrongs that you have done to me; must abstain from recalling the plots of movies in which people like you (or, perhaps, people not like you) are shot; must not look ahead to our upcoming meeting while I am at the gun range; and must not meditate on Stalin's aphorism "No man, no problem." If performing these mental acts is within my direct control, then I am likely to be under a derivative obligation to do so, while if it is not, then I may be obligated to perform others that will in turn enable me to perform them. Because the initial prohibition will thus give rise to an expanding set of derivative obligations, my commitment to the moral scheme that imposes it will indeed limit the range of options that I see as open to me.

As it happens, relatively few moralists take morality to regulate even the stray thoughts that sometimes pop into people's heads. However, the same reasoning that shows that prohibitions against thoughts of this type would lead to others will also show this about the sorts of prohibitions that many moralists do accept. Because that reasoning plays out differently when the prohibited thoughts are ones that would arise through association and when they would be based on evidence, I will address each possibility separately. However, in each case, the central idea is that a prohibition against any single thought is bound to diffuse itself, like dye poured into water, among many others.

Let's begin with prohibitions against unsavory attitudes and fantasies, and let's suppose that a certain agent—Solenz will again do nicely—is prone to a rich array of these. We may suppose, in particular, that quite apart from nursing his perpetual grudge against Putterbaugh, Solenz is given to reveries about dandling prepubescent girls, is subject to fits of intense jealousy when others are successful, and seethes with resentment at the slightest of slights. However, let's suppose as well that Solenz accepts a moral code that condemns these fantasies and attitudes as wrong, takes his moral obligations seriously, and has lived with himself long enough to know when the forbidden thoughts are likely to arise. He knows, for example, that thinking of a certain friend will lead to fantasies about the friend's daughter, that recalling a coworker's recent promotion will reawaken both his jealousy and his resentment at being passed over, and that simply imagining Putterbaugh's placid contentment will elicit wave after wave of raw malice.

Knowing all this, Solenz must be subject to a variety of self-imposed restrictions. Because his internalized moral commitments prohibit the creepy thoughts and unseemly feelings to which he is prone, they must also require that he avoid whichever more innocent thoughts are sufficiently likely to lead to those thoughts and feelings. This means not only that he must resist thinking about his friend, his colleague, and his neighbor, but also that he must actively monitor the likely associative paths from whatever else he is currently thinking about, and must constantly be at the ready to reorient his thoughts in safer directions ("Think of England"). Also, of course, because Solenz is likely to know of many other young girls, to have met many other successful people, and to feel that he has suffered many other slights, the range of thoughts that he must avoid, and of associative pathways against which he must guard, will also expand accordingly.

When one thought leads to another by association, the relation between them is causal but not normative. Although association has its own "logic," the fact that someone has the first of two associated thoughts implies neither that he has any reason to have the second nor that anything is amiss if he does not. By contrast, when one belief gives rise to another by providing evidence for it, the relation between the two beliefs is both normative *and* causal. If someone believes both p and if p then q, and as a result also believes q, then he both (1) has reason to believe q and (2) is caused to believe q by his having that reason. Just how the evidential and causal relations between a person's beliefs are themselves related is one of the deepest questions in the philosophy of mind.

But, fortunately, we don't need to answer that question to see how a prohibition against any one belief can again give rise to prohibitions against numerous others. To illustrate this in a way that parallels what was just said, let us now suppose that we are morally forbidden to hold certain beliefs. Taking our cue from some recent literature on partiality, let us suppose that it is wrong to believe that one's friend or child is guilty of the crime of which he is accused.[5] In addition, taking our cue from those who sought Lawrence Summers's resignation as president of Harvard, let us suppose that it is wrong to believe that the ability to engage in high-level abstract reasoning may be statistically more common in men than in women. (For brevity, I will sometimes express this as the belief that women and men are not equally good at

[5] For relevant discussion, see Sarah Stroud, "Epistemic Partiality in Friendship," *Ethics* 116, no. 3 (April 2006), pp. 498–524; Simon Keller, "Belief for Someone Else's Sake," *Philosophical Topics* 46, no. 1 (Spring 2018), pp. 19–35; and Anthony Carreras, "Amicably Deceived," *Philosophical Papers* 45, nos. 1–2, pp. 133–58. Although these authors agree that we are sometimes required to disregard or downplay certain sorts of evidence, it is not always clear whether they take this requirement to be a moral one.

everything.) Insofar as what we believe is causally dependent on our evidence, it will be hard if not impossible to avoid holding either of these beliefs if we think we have good enough evidence for it. Thus, if we are morally required to believe that our child is innocent of a crime, then we will also be required to downgrade or reject whatever evidence might tell for his guilt, and if we are morally required to view women and men as equally good at everything, then we will also be required to downgrade or reject whatever evidence might suggest that they are not. By extension, we will also be required to downgrade or reject the evidence for our evidence, the evidence for our evidence for our evidence, and so on. In this way, a prohibition against any single belief will again ramify to encompass prohibitions against numerous others.

III

In mounting these arguments, I have been assuming that agents who are morally committed to avoiding particular thoughts can sometimes know which mental acts or abstentions will enable them to accomplish this. If an agent cannot see how to block a forbidden thought, then his commitment to the thought's wrongness will give him no reason to regard any options as closed to him. But if an agent does recognize that a certain mental activity would make him less likely to have a forbidden thought, then hasn't he in effect already *had* that thought? And, if he has, then won't the idea that he can avoid having it by performing the relevant mental acts be a nonstarter?

If this seductive objection worked, it would block my claim that accepting a prohibition on any given type of thought means accepting a further set of derivative prohibitions and requirements. But, in fact, the objection does not work, and to see why, we need only look more closely at its premise that recognizing what would cause one to have a forbidden thought entails actually having that thought. This premise derives its plausibility from the fact that each forbidden thought's propositional content will also be part of the content of a belief that a given mental activity would give rise to such a thought, but it is falsified by the further fact that no forbidden thought is *exhausted by* its propositional content.

For when a moralist maintains that it is wrong have a belief or attitude or fantasy in which a particular proposition is embedded—when, for example, he claims that it is wrong to believe that women are less able than men, or to take pleasure in one's awareness that another is suffering—his condemnation is directed not at the bare content of the embedded propositions <women are less able than men> and <someone is suffering>, but rather at the larger beliefs and attitudes *in which* these propositions are embedded. The moralist would not see anything wrong with believing that we lack evidence that women are less able than men, or with taking a deploring attitude toward another's suffering, despite the fact that each such belief and attitude embeds exactly the same proposition as one that he does condemn. And because what is present in an awareness of what would cause a forbidden thought is only that thought's embedded content, but not the thought itself, it is indeed possible to have the awareness without having the thought. It is one thing to expect that an extended study of what went on in the concentration camps would lead one to believe that human nature is corrupt, but quite another actually to hold that belief; one thing to recognize that such a study would make one a misanthrope, but quite another actually to be one; and one thing to recognize that the study would issue in cruel fantasies, but quite another actually to have them.

Because it is possible to recognize that a given mental action would reduce one's likelihood of having a forbidden belief, attitude, or fantasy without actually having that belief, attitude, or fantasy, there is nothing self-defeating about trying to avoid having it by performing the mental action. Thus, at least where beliefs, attitudes, and fantasies are concerned, my claim that prohibitions ramify in ways that limit our mental freedom remains undefeated. Moreover, although it may be less obvious, essentially the same point holds for prohibitions against the simpler ugly thoughts that sometimes pop up in each person's mind. Even if few moralists care much about the moral status of these transient thoughts, it remains worth noting that they too involve more than just the content they share with beliefs about their causes.

For no less than each particular belief, attitude, or fantasy, each momentary ugly thought—each transient impulse to shoot you, image of you bleeding on the floor, and surge of delight at the thought of your death—will in its freestanding form have various features that are absent from the recognition that a given mental action would block a thought of that type. Where the impulse to shoot you is concerned, the additional feature is its connection to my motivational system, while where the image and the feeling are concerned, it's their phenomenal content. Because we can be aware of what would cause us to have each type of forbidden thought without actually *having* a thought of that type, our commitment to avoiding such thoughts may indeed give rise to various derivative commitments to avoiding their causes. And, hence, whatever threats to freedom of mind are posed by ramifying prohibitions against beliefs, attitudes, and fantasies will also be posed by ramifying prohibitions against stray ugly thoughts.

IV

But how great, really, is the threat that any of these prohibitions pose? At first glance, the answer may appear to be "not very," since far from being anomalous, restrictions on options are a universal condition of life. Of the innumerable restrictions that each person faces, many are imposed by his physical limitations, many others by contingencies that limit his opportunities, and many others again by the social and legal system under which he lives. Far from depriving us of freedom, these limitations are a necessary backdrop for its exercise; for to act freely is always to choose among sets of options which at the moment are not themselves up for choice.[6] It is true that someone can lack freedom because his option range is too small or insufficiently varied, but once we get above a certain threshold, our freedom no longer depends on the number or variety of our options.[7] We don't become significantly less free when our options are reduced because our neighborhood

---

[6] For elaboration and defense of these claims, see the chapter entitled "Coping with Contingency" (ch. 7) of my book *Equality for Inegalitarians* (Cambridge: Cambridge University Press, 2014).

[7] For important discussion of these issues, see Charles Taylor, "What's Wrong with Negative Liberty," in his *Philosophy and the Human Sciences: Philosophical Papers 2* (Cambridge: Cambridge University Press, 1985), and Joseph Raz, *The Morality of Freedom* (Oxford: Oxford University Press, 1986), ch. 14 and passim.

supermarket has closed, the city has started charging for street parking, or we have to give up jogging because our knees are giving out. We also don't lose any freedom of any significance when the government, or our conscience, deprives us of the option of raping or killing without paying a heavy penalty.

But why, in that case, should our loss be any more significant when our moral commitments deprive us either of the option of having morally forbidden thoughts or of the option of abstaining from the sorts of mental activities that are likely to prevent them? Just as someone who lacks the option of killing without penalty remains able to do many other things, someone who lacks the option of *thinking* of killing retains a vast field of other things to think about. And, in light of this, won't the person who takes himself to lack the option of thinking a forbidden thought still retain all the mental freedom that matters?

The answer, I think, is that he will not, but to see why, we must focus not on how his moral commitment affects the number or variety of his options, but rather on how it affects their content or quality. What's really threatening to mental freedom about a ramifying set of constraints on thought is not that they would leave us with too little to think about but that they would leave us unable to think about anything in a whole-hearted and uninhibited way. They would inhibit our mental agency by requiring both that we run each memory, fantasy, and conjecture through a series of filters before we give ourselves over to it and that we remain constantly at the ready to alter course if things start to move in a forbidden direction. The main way in which these requirements would compromise our freedom is not by limiting the range of things that we can think about but by restricting our ability to follow our thoughts wherever they lead.

When it is described at this level of generality, the difficulty is one that arises both for prohibitions against nonrational mental activities such as remembering, contemplating, and fantasizing and for the sorts of activities in which we engage when we are trying to arrive at true beliefs or avoid false ones. However, when we narrow our focus, we encounter important differences in the ways in which the two classes of prohibitions limit our freedom. To bring this out, it will again be helpful to examine each class of prohibitions separately.

Where nonrational mental activities such as contemplating and remembering are concerned, we may at first seem able to avoid the need to be perpetually on guard by simply choosing not to contemplate or remember anything that we know to be forbidden. But this won't solve the problem because anything that we do choose to contemplate or remember will be associated in our minds with various other things, and whatever control we exercise by restricting our attention to the safe subject will not extend to the thoughts that are associated with it. The danger against which the moralist must guard is that of being brought up short by a sudden awareness that what he has innocently chosen to think about is linked by association to thoughts that are not innocent at all. Each person's mental life is a continuous sequence of thoughts and feelings of unutterable complexity, and no one is in a position to know which ones have gotten stuck together in his own head. Because we can never rule out the possibility that any thought will lead to any other—because thought swoops and darts—there is no gap of logic or relevance that cannot be crossed in an instant. Thus, for someone who takes seriously the need to head off any thought that will trigger a forbidden fantasy or emotional reaction, every mental act will be a first step into a moral minefield.

An analogy will be helpful here. In a time like ours, in which so much of life has been politicized and political passions run high, it is easy to say and do things that put other people's backs up; and as a result, we all proceed with caution when we're talking to people we don't know well. To avoid eliciting hostility or giving offense, we are guarded in what we say and we stick to safe subjects. This isn't always a tragedy—talking about sports can be fun—but it reduces our chances of making any real intellectual progress or real contact with our interlocutor's mind. A freewheeling conversation is organic, and we can have one only if we feel free to allow it to develop.[8] But private thought, too, is a kind of conversation—one that we have with ourselves—and it's no less vulnerable to the stultifying effects of self-imposed limits than its public counterpart.

---

[8] For illuminating discussion of these points, see Emily Fox Gordon, "How I Learned to Talk," *American Scholar* 88, no. 4 (Autumn 2019), pp. 82–93.

Because the moralist must view *all* mental acts as threatening to take him into forbidden territory, their doing so need not affect his choices among them. But even if that danger has no impact on *what* he chooses to remember or wonder about or pay attention to, it will definitely affect the *quality* of his remembering or wondering or attending. Because he must always be on the uptake for incipient transgression, the moralist can never entirely give himself over to any line of thought. His musings can never be fully spontaneous or open-ended because he must always be aware of (and, indeed, must always *be*) the internal censor who is lurking to spoil the fun. Thus, even if his range of thought options is undiminished, the moralist is not free to pursue any of them with a whole heart or an unencumbered mind.

V

So far, I have defended only my claim that if any thoughts are morally off limits, then our freedom to contemplate, remember, or otherwise direct our thoughts will be threatened by the ease with which permitted thoughts can nonrationally lead to forbidden ones. But I have also claimed that if any *beliefs* are morally off limits, then our freedom to engage in certain *rational* activities will be threatened by the ease with which they can lead to forbidden beliefs. This last claim requires a separate defense, and to provide it, I must explain both which rational activities I have in mind and exactly how moralism about the mental threatens our freedom to engage in them.

Because we arrive at beliefs by making inferences and drawing conclusions from our evidence, it would be natural to suppose that inferring and drawing conclusions are the rational activities whose freedom I take to be threatened by prohibitions on beliefs. However, in fact, I don't think this, for I don't think inferring and concluding are actions at all. Despite the agential overtones of "infer" and "conclude," the transition from an evidential belief to the further belief for which it is evidence is not one that we choose to make, but rather happens automatically as soon as we recognize the evidential connection. This does not mean that our freedom to make inferences and draw conclusions is not threatened by the conviction that some beliefs are morally wrong—to the contrary, I will argue that this threat is both real and important—but it does mean that what is threatened is not our freedom to make certain choices or perform certain actions but rather the unimpeded functioning of the *process* through which we form our beliefs on the basis of evidence.

To locate a choice-related activity whose freedom can be threatened by the support that apparently innocent beliefs can lend to forbidden ones, we must shift our attention to an earlier stage of the process through which beliefs are formed. Instead of focusing on the stage at which some beliefs give rise to others, we must look to the earlier stage at which agents ask what they *should* believe about some aspect of the world. There are indefinitely many questions that we can ask, and which ones we pursue, and how we go about pursuing them, are for the most part up to us. Taking my cue from this, I now want to argue that the rational activity whose freedom is threatened by the prospect of arriving at impermissible beliefs is not inference but inquiry—not the acquisition of beliefs on the basis of evidence we already have, but rather what we do when we pose and explore the questions to which our evidence-based beliefs are the answers.[9]

The main elements of the threat that prohibitions on beliefs pose to freedom of inquiry have already been laid out. If we are not allowed to believe that our beloved child has committed a string of burglaries or that men are better at some things and women at others, then we must also be prohibited from doing anything that would cause us to form these beliefs. However, we cannot help forming beliefs on the basis of evidence, and we cannot know in advance what evidence we might acquire by (e.g.) reading the police report or examining studies of the relation between gender and performance. Thus, if we are obligated to believe that our child is innocent and that women and men are equally good at everything, then we cannot embark on either inquiry without running the risk of acquiring a forbidden belief. This risk threatens our freedom of inquiry in at least two ways.

---

[9] For a penetrating defense of the claims that forming a belief is always answering some sort of question, and that this is what explains why we can't choose to believe one thing rather than another, see Pamela Hieronymi, "Responsibility for Believing," *Synthese* 161 (2008), pp. 357–73.

The first and most obvious threat is simply that we may regard the risk as too great to be morally justified. If we think both that the beliefs in question are seriously wrong and that many other questions are more worthy of our attention, then we may view the moral risks that are posed by reading the police report or the psychological studies as impermissibly high. If we do, then we will not be free to investigate because our own moral commitments will prevent us from doing so.[10] Moreover, even if we initially view these risks as acceptable (perhaps because we hope that running them will allow us to discredit the forbidden beliefs once and for all), we may be brought up short if the early returns are not favorable. If we realize that the police report or the psychological studies are trending in the direction of supporting a belief that we must not have, then the only way to avoid acquiring that belief will be to stop reading. Thus, no less than the nonrational forms of mental activity that were discussed earlier, any rational inquiry that can lead us into forbidden territory will for that very reason be subject to cancellation at any moment.

And like our nonrational mental activities, too, our rational inquiries are *always* capable of leading us into forbidden territory. They are always capable of doing this not only for the reason cited earlier—that any thought can lead by association to any other—but also because there are no limits on where any investigation may lead. Everything we now believe stands in a variety of evidential and probabilistic and logical relations to innumerable other beliefs, and new beliefs are coming into the system all the time. Because we are aware of only the tiniest fraction of these connections, the probing intellect will constantly be readjusting the system as it discovers others, and any of these adjustments may lead the moralist where he doesn't want to go. Knowing this, the moralist will be inhibited and cautious: he won't be able to speculate freely for fear of transgressing, and that will reduce his ability to process not only the evidence for beliefs that are forbidden, but also the evidence for beliefs that are not. Although George Orwell's topic was censorship under totalitarianism rather than moral

---

[10] For a defense of the view that scientists should indeed refrain from investigating questions whose answers might prove damaging to disadvantaged groups, see Philip Kitcher, *Science, Truth, and Democracy* (Oxford: Oxford University Press, 2001).

constraints on thought, he elegantly summarized the general point when he wrote that "[e]ven a single taboo can have an all-around crippling effect upon the mind because there is always the danger that any thought which is freely followed up may lead to the forbidden thought."[11]

VI

Orwell's point, and mine, is that constraints on belief undercut freedom of mind by inhibiting inquiries that might provide evidence for forbidden beliefs. To say that we might have evidence for a forbidden belief is to presuppose that what would count as evidence for a belief is independent of whether we are morally permitted to hold it—that the belief's epistemic status is one thing and its moral status quite another. Recently, however, a number of philosophers have rejected this presupposition and have replaced it with the view that the standards of evidence are themselves affected by a belief's moral status. On their view, it takes more to justify a belief when accepting it would mean wronging someone than when it would not. Because this view imports moral considerations into what used to be a separate epistemic field, the phenomenon it purports to designate has become known as "moral encroachment."

The relation between moral encroachment and the argument of this book is a matter of some delicacy. On the one hand, because the book's overall thesis is that no beliefs are morally wrong, it would beg the question to base an objection to that thesis on a view that presupposes that some beliefs *are* morally wrong. However, on the other hand, the unfolding positive argument for my thesis is that prohibitions on thoughts would compromise our freedom of mind by preventing us from matching our beliefs to our evidence; and when the claim that some beliefs are morally wrong

---

[11] George Orwell, "The Prevention of Literature," in Sonia Orwell and Ian Angus, eds., *The Collected Essays, Journalism and Letters of George Orwell*, vol. 4 (London: Secker and Warburg, 1968), p. 65. For elaboration of Orwell's point as it applies to feminist demands for solidarity, see Emily Fox Gordon, "Against Solidarity," *American Scholar* 86, no. 4 (2017), pp. 61–75.

is used only to block that argument, it can be introduced simply as the antecedent of a conditional. Although the proponents of moral encroachment are in fact a highly moralistic bunch, all they would need to show to counter my freedom-of-mind argument is *if* any beliefs are morally wrong, then we can reject those beliefs without going against the evidence for them because the very fact that they are morally wrong raises the evidential bar to a point that the evidence cannot reach. As long as it is used only in this way, the claim that some beliefs are morally wrong will *not* beg the question against my overall argument.

We may well wonder, though, why we should *accept* the view that the standards of evidence for beliefs vary with their moral status. When proponents of moral encroachment advance this view, they sometimes appear to do so on the grounds that we need to accept it in order to be able to criticize those whose morally objectionable beliefs are well supported by evidence of the standard sort. Along these lines, Rima Basu and Mark Schroeder have written:

> So long as the bar for sufficiency of evidence does not depend on moral factors, it follows that the epistemic requirements governing belief cannot be sensitive to moral considerations. So it is no wonder that evidentialists have not believed that we can wrong one another in virtue of what we believe about one another.
>
> But we infer, in contrast, that the bar for sufficiency of evidence *does* depend on moral factors. As the moral considerations against belief increase, so does the evidence that is required in order to epistemically justify that belief.[12]

On this account, the rationale for the moral encroachment thesis appears to be simply that without it we will have no basis for condemning those who hold beliefs that obviously *warrant* our condemnation.

---

[12] Rima Basu and Mark Schroeder, "Doxastic Wronging," in Brian Kim and Matthew McGrath, eds., *Pragmatic Encroachment in Epistemology* (New York: Routledge, 2019), pp. 201–2; emphasis in original. For a similar but more tentative suggestion, see Stroud, "Epistemic Partiality in Friendship," p. 522.

Even on its own terms, this rationale seems problematic; for even if the strength of the evidence that we would need to justify a given belief does increase with the wrongness of holding that belief, there will still be a question about why we can never have evidence that is strong enough to meet even the heightened standard.[13] However, for present purposes, we need not pursue that question because a more decisive rejoinder is available: namely, that within this defense of the moral encroachment thesis, the claim that some beliefs are morally wrong is advanced categorically rather than as the antecedent of a conditional. To establish that what would ordinarily be good evidence is not sufficient to support a racist or sexist belief, Basu and Schroeder cannot simply assume for purposes of argument that that belief is morally wrong; for because that assumption could also be made about any other belief, it would not explain why the justification of this belief in particular must meet a heightened standard. To have any hope of showing this, Basu and Schroeder must assert that beliefs of the relevant sorts *actually are* morally wrong, and given their broader reprobative proclivities, that clearly is what they have in mind. However, in the context of the present discussion, whose guiding question is precisely whether any beliefs *are* morally wrong, any defense of moral encroachment which itself assumed that some beliefs are morally wrong would move the appeal to that thesis squarely back into question-begging territory.

VII

The question that we must ask, therefore, is whether there is any plausible way of defending the moral encroachment thesis that does *not* assume that some beliefs are morally wrong; and to assess that possibility, it will be helpful to turn our attention to the closely related thesis

---

[13] Concerning the possibility of "cases of belief that are rational in every way required for knowledge but are nevertheless morally wrong," Basu and Schroeder roundly assert, "[W]e believe that there are no such cases" ("Doxastic Wrongdoing," p. 197). To square this assertion with their claim that the evidence that is required for knowledge increases with the moral considerations against a belief, one would have to take the latter claim to assert that the increase in the strength of the evidence that is required is not gradual, but rather that the requisite level jumps straight up to infinity as soon as the moral case against holding the belief reaches some (which?) crucial point.

of *pragmatic* encroachment. This thesis asserts that the strength of the evidence that is needed to justify a belief varies with the *practical* consequences of holding it—that, for example, we need less evidence to justify the belief that a flimsy table will support twenty pounds of books than we do to justify the belief that it will support twenty pounds of baby. Although some aspects of pragmatic encroachment are themselves controversial,[14] there is clearly something to it, and it is prima facie relevant to our topic because moral reasons are often viewed as a subclass of practical ones. Thus, we may be tempted to suppose that whatever case can be made for the thesis of pragmatic encroachment can simply be carried over to its moral cousin.[15]

But problems with this supposition emerge as soon as we ask *why* the strength of the evidence that is needed to justify a belief should vary with the consequences of holding it. The obvious answer is that what we believe affects the way we pursue our goals, and that the consequences of acting on some false beliefs are much worse than those of acting on others. There is little harm in acting on the false belief that the table will support the books but much harm in acting on the false belief that it will support the baby, and this is what explains why the latter belief requires more in the way of justification. Thus, to mount a parallel argument for moral encroachment, one would have to argue that the harm that will ensue if the relevant moral beliefs are false is also great enough to raise the evidential bar.

But is it? There are a number of problems with this argument, the first of which is simply that its factual premise is a poor fit with many

<hr />

[14] One contested question is whether the opinions that need more justification when the stakes are high are restricted to full beliefs, or whether they also or instead include credences, probabilistic beliefs, or knowledge. Another is whether we can accept both pragmatic encroachment and evidentialism. For discussion of the first question, see Sarah Moss, "Moral Encroachment," *Proceedings of the Aristotelian Society* 118, part 2, pp. 177–205. For opposing views on the second question, see Richard Foley, "Epistemically Rational Belief and Responsible Belief," in R. Cobb-Stevens, ed., *Proceedings of the Twentieth World Congress of Philosophy* (Bowling Green, OH: Philosophy Documentation Center, 2000) and Jeremy Fantl and Matthew McGrath, "Evidence, Pragmatics, and Justification," *Philosophical Review* 111, no. 1 (January 2002), pp. 67–94.

[15] For argument along these lines, see James Fritz, "Pragmatic Encroachment and Moral Encroachment," *Pacific Philosophical Quarterly* 98, no. 1 (December 2017), pp. 643–61, and Michael Pace, "The Epistemic Value of Moral Considerations: Justification, Moral Encroachment, and James' 'Will to Believe,'" *Nous* 45, no. 2 (2011), pp. 239–68.

of the beliefs that the actual proponents of moral encroachment have taken to raise the evidential stakes. Within that literature, we are said to wrong someone when we believe that

1. an applicant for employment at a social-justice-oriented think tank would be a poor fit because he previously worked for a hedge fund;[16] that
2. our partner has forgotten to pick up a prescription which in fact was not yet ready;[17] that
3. the Black diner whom we are serving will not tip well;[18] that
4. a female employee at a firm we are visiting is an administrative assistant rather than an executive;[19] and that
5. Rajeev smells of curry.[20]

Of these beliefs, some might result in some minor harm if they were acted on, but with the possible exception of the first (which might keep the best applicant from being hired), none would have any impact of any real significance. Thus, unlike the sorts of beliefs that if acted on might cause real damage—a concussion to the baby, the sinking of the ship in Clifford's famous example[21]—none of them can be expected to raise the evidential bar to a point that the evidence cannot reach.

Considered by itself, this objection is not decisive. To respond, a defender of the parallel between pragmatic and moral encroachment might first narrow his focus to beliefs that are rooted in bias and then appeal to the major harms that are caused by societal racism and the other pervasive forms of bias to which each such belief contributes.[22]

---

[16] Kate Nolfi, "Moral Agency in Believing," *Philosophical Topics* 46, no. 1 (Spring 2018), pp. 55–56.

[17] Ibid.

[18] Rima Basu, "The Wrongs of Racist Beliefs," *Philosophical Studies*, forthcoming.

[19] Adapted by Georgi Gardiner, "Evidentialism and Moral Encroachment" in Kevin McCain, ed., *"Believing in Accordance with the Evidence: New Essays on Evidentialism* (Cham, Switzerland: Springer, forthcoming) from an example on Sarah Moss, *Probabilistic Knowledge* (Oxford: Oxford University Press, 2018).

[20] Basu, "The Wrongs of Racist Beliefs."

[21] The example, which appears in the title essay of William K. Clifford, *The Ethics of Belief and Other Essays* (Amherst, NY: Prometheus Books, 1999), concerns a shipowner who allows his ship to sail despite evidence that it may not be seaworthy.

[22] I don't know of any defender of the parallel who has explicitly made the first move, but Mark Schroeder appears to make the second when he writes that "a false belief that a

However, quite apart from making the moral encroachment thesis far less interesting by drastically narrowing its scope, this rejoinder would raise a number of further questions. It would require an explanation of why the tiny additional harm that a single biased belief would contribute to the overall total should warrant a major elevation in the standards for that belief's justification. It would also need to be backed by an explanation of why a biased belief should be expected to cause any harm at all if the person who holds it both believes that expressing or otherwise acting on it would be wrong and has a normal level of self-control.

Moreover, even if both of these challenges could be overcome, a further and still more serious problem would remain. The basic difficulty with the attempt to assimilate moral encroachment to pragmatic encroachment is that whereas under pragmatic encroachment the standards of justification go up when a belief would lead to serious harm *if it were false*, the rationale for elevating the standards of justification for biased or stereotyped beliefs has little do with their truth or falsity. Whatever is thought to be damaging about these beliefs would still be thought to be damaging if the job applicant were in fact a poor fit, if the Black diner were in fact a poor tipper, and if Rajeev did in fact smell of curry.[23] Thus, the problem with these beliefs cannot be that their objects would suffer serious physical, economic, or emotional harm if the beliefs turned out to be false, but must instead be that there is a kind of moral harm that these individuals suffer simply by *being* the objects of the beliefs.

But if the problem is that people are wronged, and so harmed, simply by being the objects of biased or stereotyped beliefs, then the parallel between pragmatic and moral encroachment will collapse; for if the relevant harms would be suffered whether or not the beliefs were false, then there is no point in elevating the standards of justification

black man is staff not only diminishes him, but diminishes him in a way that aggravates an accumulated store of past injustice." Mark Schroeder, "Rational Stability under Pragmatic Encroachment," *Episteme*, forthcoming, quoted in Gardiner, "Evidentialism and Moral Encroachment."

[23] I owe my appreciation of this important point to Moss, "Moral Encroachment," pp. 194ff.; see also Basu, "The Wrongs of Racist Beliefs."

to make sure that the beliefs are *not* false. Moreover, quite apart from this, any argument which sought to preserve the parallel between the two forms of encroachment by relying on a conception of harm that presupposed the moral wrongness of biased or stereotyped beliefs would be dialectically inappropriate. If the parallel between moral and pragmatic encroachment did require such a conception of harm, then anyone who first defended moral encroachment by invoking the parallel and then used moral encroachment to block my defense of the claim that no thoughts are morally wrong would again be begging the question against my central claim.

VIII

This completes my discussion of the ways in which internalized constraints on thought would threaten our freedom to perform mental actions. They would do so, I have argued, by imposing a chilling vigilance on all the different kinds of mental activity that might lead to the forbidden thoughts—that is, on all mental activities, period. But what, next, of thoughts that *don't* involve mental activity? Inferring and making associative connections aren't things we choose to do, so we can't be rendered less free to choose to do them by our fear of violating moral prohibitions. Instead, when an internalized moral constraint renders a transition of this sort unfree, it does so by distorting some relevant causal process.

To see how this works, consider again the person who thinks it wrong to believe that women and men are not equally good at everything, but who holds a number of other beliefs which by ordinary standards would be sufficient to justify that belief. Although it's not essential, let's assume that these other beliefs are not rooted in bias or malice and have not been arrived at lightly: they are informed by the person's keen awareness of gender disparities in the professions, his careful reading of studies that purport to record gender-based differences in performance and to offer physiological explanations of these differences, his attentive observation of the different playing styles of young children of different genders, and his reluctant inability to accept attempts to attribute the disparities to differences in socialization or oppressive social institutions. For present purposes, it doesn't matter whether his beliefs are true or false; the point is simply that he has them, and the question that their conflict with his moral commitments raises is "Where do his thoughts go?"

There are, I think, a number of possibilities. When someone is morally committed to believing that women and men are equally good at everything but also holds beliefs that strongly suggest that they're not, one thing that can happen is that he simply holds on to all of the inconsistent beliefs without clearly registering the conflicts among them.[24] If the conflict is uncomfortable enough, his mind may simply blur it. Alternatively, if he does register the inconsistency, he may be unsure about which of his beliefs should be retained and which abandoned. However, if he is both clear-headed and fully committed to morality as he understands it—for the moralist, the ideal combination—then he will not react with uncertainty. In that case, instead of making the usual automatic transition from his evidential beliefs to the conclusion that women and men are not equally good at everything, he will move just as automatically from his unshakable conviction that women and men *are* equally good at everything to an outright rejection of some (possibly indeterminate) subset of his conflicting beliefs. Instead of delivering up a modus ponens, the automatic inferential process will yield a modus tollens. Because many of the beliefs that he will be moved to abandon are themselves likely to be held for reasons—because, for example, his confidence in the studies he has read may be rooted in his beliefs that the journals are selective and the authors reputable—some of these revisions in his evidential beliefs are likely to lead to others. But eventually a new equilibrium will be reached.

At first glance, this last process may not seem particularly unusual, for it bears a superficial resemblance to what happens when *any* belief is rejected because it conflicts with other things we believe. However, in the standard case, the system readjusts itself in response to (what the

---

[24] For an account of self-deception that turns on the motivating force of desire, and so can accommodate such failures of recognition, see Alfred Mele, *Self-Deception Unmasked* (Princeton, NJ: Princeton University Press, 2001). For a chilling account of the phenomenology of this form of self-deception, see the treatment of doublethink in George Orwell's *1984* (New York: Harcourt Brace, 1949), esp. pp. 220–23, 287–89, and passim.

person regards as) the relative strengths of the reasons for and against the competing beliefs. By contrast, when a moralist rejects the evidence for a belief that he regards as forbidden, he does so not because he thinks the overall balance of evidence dictates its rejection but because of a commitment that does not make contact with the evidence at all.[25] When someone's thought moves backward in this way, the natural process of inference is blocked or distorted.

Earlier I compared a moral commitment that disrupts what would otherwise be the natural flow of a person's ideas to a beaver dam that diverts the course of a freely flowing river, and the force of that analogy as it pertains to inference should now be clear. Just as the dam causes the water to back up rather than continuing to flow downstream, a prohibition on belief causes the stream of inference to back up onto itself. Instead of moving forward from the evidence for the forbidden belief to its acceptance, the stream either moves backward from the forbidden belief's rejection to the rejection of the evidence for it or else escapes its banks and flows into a spreading pool that lacks boundaries or structure. In either case, because the normal channels of inference are defined *by* the requirements of reason, the freedom that is lost is precisely that of forming one's beliefs in *accordance* with reason.

The analogy doesn't work quite as neatly when the thoughts that a person views as forbidden consist of attitudes, emotions, fantasies, or desires, for although many such mental occurrences do have significant cognitive content, and can to that extent be assessed as rational or irrational, the same cognitive content can belong to attitudes and fantasies that are marked by many different combinations of affect and desire. An awareness of danger may be coupled with fear in one person but with excitement in another. Although the issue remains controversial, I take this to show that the causal paths that lead to the affective and conative components of these mixed mental states are not dictated by norms of rationality. If I am right about this, then the freedom

---

[25] The issue here is clouded by the fact that the person may indeed have evidence (in the broad sense of beliefs that he takes to supply a justification) for his moral commitment itself. However, whatever that evidence implies about the truth of the moral principle to which he is committed, it obviously has no bearing on the truth of any belief that that principle forbids (or, therefore, on the truth of any belief that provides evidence *for* any forbidden belief). It is only these beliefs whose rejection is not based on evidence.

that someone loses when his moral commitments prevent him from acquiring a nasty attitude, or from feeling a vicious emotion or drifting into an ugly fantasy, can hardly be the freedom to acquire his attitudes, feelings, or fantasies in a way that *accords* with reason.

Yet even if it is not, the disruption of the relevant causal process can still be seen to undermine his freedom in a closely related way. As we saw in Chapter 4, although a person's vicious attitudes, emotions, and fantasies need not be manifestations of any corresponding broad-gauged vices, they must indeed result from the interplay of some subset of the beliefs, attitudes, values, and dispositions that collectively make up his character. Because of this, any internalized moral prohibition that prevents him from acquiring a given attitude, emotion, or fantasy must do so by blocking the usual effects of certain aspects of his character. At least to this extent, the blocked-stream analogy continues to hold. Moreover, by thus interfering with a causal sequence that would otherwise originate in the person's character, the internalized prohibition must prevent a part of his nature from expressing itself. This may in some ways be a good thing—I will consider this possibility in the next chapter—but even if it is, it will curtail his mental freedom by leaving him less free to be himself.

7

Encomium

In the previous chapter, I argued that internalized prohibitions on thought compromise our freedom in various ways. To complete my argument, I must now explain why these losses of freedom matter. This requires exploring the connections between mental freedom and human well-being, and that is my agenda in this concluding chapter. By pursuing it, I hope not only to make a positive case for freedom of mind that is strong enough to outweigh any residual case for moralism about the mental, but also to bring out what is beautiful about the freedom to think even the ugliest of thoughts.

I

I have argued that internalized constraints on thought restrict our freedom in at least four ways. They do so, I suggested, by (1) preventing us from choosing to press certain lines of inquiry; (2) interfering with the causal processes through which beliefs are normally acquired, retained, or abandoned; (3) distorting the natural play of our emotions, attitudes, and fantasies; and (4) limiting what we choose to remember, reflect on, and fantasize about. The question that remains to be answered is how any of this makes our lives worse.

Let's begin with the cost of not being able to follow an inquiry through. Knowledge is valuable both in itself and as a means to the effective pursuit of our goals, so one obvious cost of not being able to pursue inquiries that lead in forbidden directions is the loss of whatever knowledge they might have yielded. Inquiry is by nature unpredictable and there is no telling in advance where it will lead,[1] so

---

[1] As Alasdair MacIntyre has observed, "[a]ny invention, any discovery, which consists essentially in the elaboration of a radically new concept cannot be predicted, for a necessary part of the prediction is the present elaboration of the very concept whose discovery

when a line of thought is shut down, the knowledge that is lost often extends far beyond the answer to the original question. That loss is amplified, moreover, by the general dampening effect that internalized prohibitions on belief are bound to have on our intellectual curiosity. Quite apart from depriving us of the sense of open horizons that is one of the great rewards of intellectual endeavor, this dampening can be expected to prevent many promising lines of inquiry from even getting started.

These considerations suggest that a person's unwillingness to pursue inquiries that might lead him to acquire forbidden beliefs can significantly reduce the accuracy and completeness of his picture of the world. More important than this, however, is the negative impact that his unwillingness to pursue those inquiries will have on *him*. Quite apart from any reduction in what he can know, his unwillingness to embrace the forbidden beliefs will worsen his life in a number of further ways.

It will, for one thing, place him in an untenable relation to truth itself. Whatever else we say, we must acknowledge that we live in a world that is independent of us and whose basic features answer neither to our will nor to morality's demands. Incorporating this basic fact into our belief-system is necessary both if we are to change the world and if we are to accommodate ourselves to it: it is, indeed, a prerequisite for sanity itself. But the person who refuses to pursue a line of inquiry because he expects it to support a belief that he is not permitted to hold is precisely *not* incorporating this fact into his belief-system. He is, if only for the moment, relinquishing his grip on the reality principle. This is not likely to work over the longer haul—facts are, as they say, stubborn things—but that's not the point here. My point, rather, is that any morality that requires us to take the stance of a fabulist or fantasist is, precisely to that extent, depriving us of the essential human good of connectedness to the real world.

That world is often an ugly place, and the beliefs that moralists take us to be obligated to accept are generally much more pleasant than

_____

or invention was to take place only in the future. The notion of the prediction of radical conceptual innovation is itself conceptually incoherent." Alasdair MacIntyre, *After Virtue* (Notre Dame, IN: University of Notre Dame Press, 1981), p. 93.

the ones they think we must reject. Many would find it disturbing to think that their child has committed a crime, that women and men are not equal in all relevant dimensions, or that their partner did not care enough to remember to pick up their prescription. Because these beliefs are unpleasant, it takes a certain courage to hold them. This doesn't mean that it is cowardly *not* to hold the beliefs, but it does mean that those who do not flinch from accepting them are manifesting a virtue from which their moralistic counterparts are conveniently excused. Nietzsche maintained that it is admirable to "sacrifice desirability to truth, *every* truth, even a plain, bitter, ugly, foul, unchristian, immoral truth,"[2] and I think he was right. Kant maintained that "[i]mmaturity is the inability to use one's own understanding without the guidance of another,"[3] and I think he was right too. Facing up to the disturbing truths that morality requires us to blink away is both a way of making the type of sacrifice that Nietzsche rightly admired and a way of displaying the maturity of judgment that Kant identified as the spirit of enlightenment. These are both elements of desirable lives, and they are two more aspects of what we lose when we turn away from inquiries that lead in forbidden directions.

And there is yet a further cost, for by giving morality a veto over our intellectual endeavors, we limit our ability to claim ownership of any beliefs that ensue. Although we cannot control the outcomes of our inquiries, we can at least control the ways in which we conduct them, and quite apart from the value of having an accurate picture of the world, there is further value in having arrived at one's picture entirely by oneself. Just as the view from the top of a mountain is more valuable if one has climbed the mountain than if one has helicoptered in, a belief that someone has acquired by thinking things through on his own is more valuable than one that has been imposed from without. Even if the content of the two beliefs is identical, the first is rooted in the person's own cognitive activity, and so is fully his own, in a way that the second is not. This doesn't mean that we should never defer to anyone

---

[2] Friedrich Nietzsche, *On the Genealogy of Morality*, trans. Carol Diethe (Cambridge: Cambridge University Press, 2006), p. 11.

[3] Immanuel Kant, "An Answer to the Question: 'What Is Enlightenment?,'" in Hans Reiss, ed., *Kant's Political Writings* (Cambridge: Cambridge University Press, 1971), p. 54.

else's judgment, but it does mean that when we do, it should only be because we ourselves have judged that the other's judgment on a certain matter is more reliable than our own. However, when we abandon an inquiry in order to avoid acquiring a belief that we regard as impermissible, we are evidently *not* trying to increase the likelihood that we will arrive at the truth; for if we thought the impermissible belief was likely to be false, then we would not think it necessary to abandon our inquiry in the first place.

II

Inquiry is a voluntary activity, and the kind of freedom whose value I have been discussing is the freedom to engage in it. But internalized restrictions on belief can also distort our *non*voluntary cognitive processes, and when they do, they deprive us of freedom of a different sort. Quite apart from their impact on our investigative choices, they also disrupt the free flow of our inferences. Whereas someone who believes both that p and that p implies q will normally infer that q, a person who holds these beliefs but thinks he is forbidden to believe that q will not draw this conclusion. Instead of coming to believe that q, he will come to believe either that not-p or else that p is open to doubt in a way that deprives it of the evidential force it would otherwise have. By thus reversing the usual direction of inference, an internalized moral commitment will further impair a person's ability to know the world as it is.

To see why rejecting one's evidence rather than accepting the conclusion it supports has this effect, we need only remind ourselves of why drawing conclusions that *are* supported by evidence generally *does* extend our knowledge. Very roughly, the reason is, first, that our evidential beliefs often arise through processes that reliably convert input from the world into true belief and, second, that the standard inferential process tends to be truth-preserving. The combination of world-input and reliability is what enables our evidential beliefs to represent reality roughly as it is, while the truth-preservingness of the standard forms of inference is what enables them to extend our knowledge.

But suppose, now, that we are prevented from acquiring a belief for which we have strong evidence by our conviction that such beliefs are impermissible. In that case, whatever belief we acquire in its place will *not* be traceable to any input from the world. Thus, barring some kind of preestablished harmony, there will simply be no connection between what morality requires us to believe and what the world is like. Even if the moral principle that requires us to hold the belief were somehow known to be true, the belief that it requires us to hold would not be, and neither, a fortiori, would any of the further propositions that we inferred from it. This reinforces my previous contention that any belief that we hold simply because we take morality to require it will degrade the accuracy of our picture of the world. Of greater relevance to inference, it implies that whenever our background beliefs rearrange themselves to *accommodate* a belief that we hold only because we take morality to require it, our picture of the world will be degraded further.

Because we normally don't choose to believe one thing rather than another, my characterization of such disruptions of the normal inferential process as a form of unfreedom may seem strained. Because the function or natural aim of the inferential process is to extend our knowledge, this characterization may draw some plausibility from the link between freedom and the ability to achieve one's aims. But there is notoriously a gap between the aims of processes that occur *within persons* and the aims of *those persons themselves*. If the natural aim of inference were as distinct from the aims of the persons in whom it occurs as are the natural aims of processes such as digestion or conception, then the fact that reversing the usual direction of inference defeats its natural aim would have little bearing on anyone's freedom.

But, in fact, I think the natural aim of inference is *not* this distinct from the aims of the persons in whom it occurs; for whereas the natural aim of a process like digestion can indeed conflict with various person-level aims (such as those of persons who want to lose weight), the same does not seem true of the natural aim of inference. Instead, whatever a person happens to want or seek, he is always more likely to get it if his inferences do succeed in extending his knowledge than if they do not. In addition, it appears to be close to a conceptual truth that no one can want his inferences to issue in ignorance or error. These considerations suggest that despite its nonvoluntary nature, the natural aim of inference can indeed be attributed to the persons in whom it occurs, and this attribution, if warranted, will at least mitigate the admitted strangeness of describing the frustration of that aim as rendering those individuals less free.

III

So far, my discussion of internalized constraints on thought has focused entirely on their negative cognitive effects. Such constraints, I have argued, reduce the accuracy of our beliefs by cutting us off from important forms of evidence. But when a person holds a belief of a type that moralists condemn—when, for example, he regards another person, or the members of another race, as morally or intellectually inferior—his holding it is often not explained by his evidence at all. Instead, the explanation may lie in his visceral dislike of the other person or race, his general misanthropy, or his unthinking acceptance of malign stereotypes. Alternatively, he may hold the biased belief because he is given to projecting his own failings onto others or is too insecure to feel good about himself without downgrading someone else. And, needless to say, there are many further possibilities.

Unlike the standard patterns of inference, these nonrational belief-forming processes are not truth-conducive. For this reason, a moral commitment that prevents them from operating is unlikely to worsen a person's life by diminishing the accuracy or completeness of his picture of the world, and neither is it likely to do so by depriving him of opportunities to face up to unpleasant reality or to think things through for himself. Nevertheless, I believe, and will now argue, that when a person's moral commitments block the nonrational processes that would otherwise cause him to acquire biased beliefs, they do significantly worsen his life in another way. Because this form of worsening is not restricted to doxastic contexts—because it occurs not only when a disrupted nonrational process would otherwise issue in a biased belief but also when it would otherwise give rise to a nasty attitude, an unseemly emotion, or a repugnant fantasy—the argument that follows will serve as a bridge between my narrow claim that internalized restrictions on thought are incompatible with freedom of belief and my broader claim that those restrictions undermine freedom of mind more generally.

As a first step toward elaborating the argument as it applies to nonrationally caused beliefs, it will be helpful to juxtapose two cases in which an internalized moral constraint prevents someone from acquiring a certain belief, the first a case in which the belief would have been acquired on the basis of evidence and the second a case in which it would have been nonrationally caused. As our example of someone who is prevented from acquiring a belief on the basis of evidence, we may again consider the person whose background beliefs support the view that men are on average better at certain things than women, but whose moral commitments forbid him to accept that view. Although I have repeatedly noted that a commitment of this sort can lead a person to reject whichever combinations of background beliefs would otherwise support the forbidden belief, I have not yet said anything about what *happens* to his background beliefs once they are rejected. In a word, what happens to them is that they disappear completely. Unlike a rejected suitor or job candidate who remains on the scene to lick his wounds, a belief that someone has rejected because it conflicts with something else he believes is simply gone. Because that belief is no longer among the person's mental states at all, it is no longer capable of exerting pressure, of either the intellectual or the causal variety, against the beliefs that he takes himself to be morally obligated to hold.[4]

But now consider, in contrast, a person whose inclination to regard women as less able than men in some important respects is rooted not in evidence but in some nonrational aspect of his personality— his general misogyny, say, or some kind of deep insecurity. Despite his flawed character, such a person may also be morally committed to believing that women and men are equally good at everything, and if he is, then he too may reject the view that their abilities differ in important ways. However, and crucially, even if his moral commitments do cause him to reject this view, the misogyny or insecurity that would

---

[4] As I noted earlier, conflicts between internalized moral commitments and evidential beliefs don't always lead to the rejection of the evidential beliefs; instead, the person may simply blur the conflict or become unsure about which of his beliefs to abandon. My point in highlighting cases in which people do reject their evidential beliefs is only to draw attention to a contrasting feature of the nonevidential cases I am about to describe.

otherwise incline him to accept it will not go away. Unlike the beliefs that constituted the first person's evidence that men and women differ in ability, which simply disappeared once his belief-system rearranged itself, the second person's misogyny or insecurity will live on to fight another day.

This difference has important implications about the impact of the internalized prohibitions on the lives of the two individuals. On the one hand, it suggests that when a person ceases to hold a belief that would be evidence for a further belief that he regards as forbidden, the resulting adjustment poses no threat to his internal integrity. After the adjustment, the elements of his belief-system will continue to hang together both with one another and with the moral scheme to which he is committed. But not so the person whose impermissible belief would be rooted in his character; for because the causes of *his* tendency to hold the forbidden belief are *not* eliminated when that tendency is prevented from taking effect, their causal thrust will remain in tension with that of his moral commitments. Even when his commitment to morality prevails, he will remain subject to the undertow of his un-vanquished misogyny or insecurity. The imperatives of character will push him in one direction, while his moral commitments pull him in another. And, because of this, the price that he pays for internalizing the constraint will be that he is divided against himself.

How great a price this is, and why anyone should be reluctant to pay it, are questions to which I will return. First, though, I want to generalize the point, which applies as naturally to internalized prohibitions against attitudes, fantasies, and emotions as it does to internalized prohibitions against beliefs. Whatever ultimately explains why a person might hate or despise the members of another race, secretly want his best friend to fail, enjoy replaying mental images of road carnage, or daydream about sexually humiliating someone who rejects him, the explanation can hardly lie in his appreciation of any reasons that *support* these attitudes, desires, or fantasies. Instead, the explanation must again be purely causal, and must again lie somewhere in the ineffably complicated interplay of the person's desires, fears, appetites, habits, memories, and stored experiences. This suggests that, like the misogyny or insecurity that inclined the person in our previous example to form a biased belief, the underlying tendencies that incline people to have nasty attitudes, ugly emotions, and disturbing fantasies will not go away if their moral commitments prevent their inclinations from taking effect. And, hence, no less than the person whose misogyny or insecurity survives the moral sanitizing of his beliefs, the person whose twisted psychology survives the suppression of his nasty attitudes, unseemly emotions, or ugly fantasies will remain divided against himself.

IV

With this much established, we can return to the question of why any of it matters. Why should anyone *mind* if his moral commitments are in conflict with the nonrational forces that would otherwise shape his private thoughts? In what coin, exactly, must the price for the internal conflict be paid?

The currency can hardly be pain or suffering, since as long as the causal push-and-pull takes place below the level of consciousness, it will not impinge on a person's experience at all. Moreover, although the idea that well-being requires harmony among the parts of the soul dates back to Plato, the prestige of its illustrious progenitor is hardly a substitute for argument. Thus, the question we must now ask is whether there is any reason for the moralist not to accept with equanimity whatever divisions there might be between a person's moral principles and his subterranean tendencies of thought.

The answer, I think, is that there is, and that that reason lies partly in the familiar value of authenticity and partly in the equally familiar value of self-knowledge. Both of these values pervade the modern sensibility: the idea that it's important just to be yourself is ubiquitous in advice columns and self-help manuals, while many a gap year and psychiatric hour have been devoted to chasing down the self that one is. Both ideas can be sources of mischief if they're used to rationalize self-involved or irresponsible behavior—here the Gauguin of Williams's famous example comes to mind—but that danger won't arise if their application is restricted to the private realm.

Any attitude, fantasy, emotion, or non-reason-based belief that a person is disposed to have is authentic in the sense of having its origins in some aspect of his character or nature, and that remains true even if he has internalized a moral prohibition that prevents him from actually having it. Of course, if someone *has* internalized such a prohibition, then his acceptance of it will presumably also be rooted in his character, but that won't alter the fact that the attitudes, fantasies, and emotions that it prevents him from having would be more closely linked to his character, and hence more authentically his own, than whatever happy-face alternatives it causes to arise in their place.

Guided by these thoughts, we may infer that part of the price we pay when our moral commitments causally shape our attitudes, fantasies, or emotions is that the contents of our consciousness are no longer expressions of our true nature. When a person is divided in this way, there is a disconnect between what's going on in his mind and the way he really is. Moreover, because the most direct route to self-understanding involves reflection on what *is* going on in one's mind, any such disconnect will diminish one's prospects for self-knowledge. If the beliefs, desires, attitudes, and emotions of which a person is aware are not reflections of what he's really like, then any conclusions about himself that he draws from them are likely to be misguided. In this way, the fact that the contents of a person's consciousness are a product of his moral commitments rather than his underlying nature will undermine not only their authenticity but also his ability to draw on them to know himself.

These claims should not be misunderstood. When I say that it's better when a person actually does think whatever nasty thoughts he is inclined to think, I don't mean that it's better to be the kind of person who *is* inclined to think nasty thoughts. I readily acknowledge that it's better, both for him and just in itself, if someone is *not* the kind of person who is inclined to fantasize about corrupting children, take secret pleasure in others' pain, or hate and despise those of different ethnicities or religions. My point is only that given the kinds of people they in fact are, the pederast, the sadist, and the bigot lose nothing, but gain something important, when their awful characters are allowed to find expression in correspondingly awful thoughts. What each gains from his recognition that he is capable of having such thoughts is insight into his own nature: the ability to say, with or without apology, "This is what I am."

V

Let me summarize the argument to this point. In the preceding sections, I argued that when a person takes himself to be morally forbidden to have certain thoughts, the costs to him are likely to include his (1) coming to hold fewer true beliefs and more false ones, (2) being sheltered from hard truths that it takes courage to acknowledge, (3) being prevented from thinking things through for himself, (4) failing to accomplish important goals that he cannot avoid having, and (5) having beliefs, attitudes, fantasies, emotions, and desires that are both (5a) inauthentic and (5b) unconducive to self-knowledge. Because these costs are substantial, the forms of mental freedom that enable us to avoid them are correspondingly valuable. Even by themselves, I think these advantages are sufficient to carry the day against any morality whose acceptance would deprive us of them.

But as important as all this is, another aspect of mental freedom is more important still. The strongest reason to treasure freedom of mind lies not in its connection to knowledge, virtue, or authenticity, but rather in what it contributes to the depth and quality of human experience. That contribution is what I take to justify the current chapter's effusive title, and in the book's concluding sections, I will explore some of the ways in which our inner lives are enriched by the absence of restrictions on what we may think, feel, or imagine. Because many of the thoughts, feelings, and imaginings that contribute the most are ones we choose to entertain, these final sections will round out my discussion by vindicating the importance of the last of the four forms of freedom that I recapitulated at the beginning of the chapter.

I have already mentioned, just in passing, the sense of intellectual openness and expansiveness that accompanies unencumbered speculation and inquiry, but that is only the smallest part of what I now have in mind. One minor but telling further example is humor. Although nothing deadens a joke more than an attempt to explain why it's funny, it is worth noting that two recurrent themes in the philosophy of humor are, first, that humor often finds its occasion in the misfortunes of others and, second, that our amusement is often rooted in our sense of superiority *to* others. Although neither pattern accounts for everything we find funny, the first obviously comes into play when we laugh at others' pratfalls, while the second is often instanced by jokes that turn on stereotypes that reflect badly on certain groups. (Here's one of the latter type that will offend only my coreligionists. Englishman: "I'm so thirsty I *must* have a beer"; Frenchman: "I'm so thirsty I *must* have some wine"; Jew: "I'm so thirsty I *must* have diabetes.") Jokes of these sorts often elicit the "that's not funny" reflex, but funny they often are, and to enjoy them, we must have thoughts of precisely the sorts that many moralists decry.[5] It is no accident that in the age of wokeness, virtually every form of pungent humor has drifted off limits, and it is instructive to enumerate the reasons why a movie like *Animal House* could never be made today.

Although the more pious among us may be willing to accept this loss, most would assent to the general proposition that that our lives are greatly enriched by humor; but there is no similar agreement about the darker types of thoughts to which humans are prone. Consider, for example, schadenfreude, an emotion with important affinities to the forms of humor just discussed. Schadenfreude, understood as pleasure in the misfortunes of others, is generally regarded as deplorable. A few moralists have attempted to give it a positive gloss by restrictively defining it as pleasure at others' *deserved* misfortune:[6] their paradigm is the pleasure that we feel when the arrogant are painfully humbled or the cruel suffer cruel fates themselves. However, although cases of this sort clearly do exist, and although they are comparatively easy to rationalize by saying that what pleases us about them is only that justice is done, they do not come close to exhausting the field. The more interesting forms of schadenfreude, and the ones on which I want to focus, are those in which the frisson of pleasure is triggered not by an awful person's getting his comeuppance but by the misfortune of someone

---

[5] As I can attest, someone who is himself a member of the stereotyped group, and who himself has precisely the characteristics on which the stereotype rests, can still be amused by a joke that turns on the stereotype. Because that person's amusement can hardly be explained by his sense of superiority to his own group's members, there must be more to jokes that turn on stereotypes than the sense of superiority they elicit. However, the point I'm making in the text would of course continue to hold even if those jokes *did* work exclusively by eliciting a sense of superiority.

[6] For accounts of this sort, see A. Ben-Ze'ev, *The Subtlety of Emotion* (Cambridge, MA: MIT Press, 2000) and J. Portmann, *When Bad Things Happen to Other People* (New York: Routledge, 2000).

who is likable or admirable or whom we simply don't know. Do I really want to say that pleasures of this sort can make our lives better?

In fact, I do, and my reason turns on their role in our psychic economy. We are all keenly aware that we are vulnerable to misfortune, and we are all to one degree or another subject to it. When we become aware of another's misfortunes, we learn that we are either no worse off than he is or are actually better off. As Nietzsche observed, learning that we are no worse off than another is pleasant because it eliminates envy: "Schadenfreude originates in the fact that, in certain respects of which he is well aware, everyone feels unwell, oppressed by care or envy or sorrow: the harm that befalls another makes him our equal, it appeases our envy."[7] By contrast, as Lucretius observed, learning that we are *better* off than someone else is pleasant because it reinforces our sense that we are doing comparatively well: we take pleasure in watching a ship founder "not because it is a joyous pleasure that anyone should be made to suffer / but because it is agreeable to see from what evils thou thyself art free."[8] Despite their differences, what both passages bring out is that schadenfreude is a way of coping with our constant awareness that we are vulnerable to life's unavoidable pains, dangers, and threats.[9] It is a needed form of solace in a hostile world. Whereas humor enriches our inner lives by providing us with enjoyment and an occasion for imaginative play, schadenfreude does so by providing a kind of consolation—one of which the moralist would deprive us for no good reason.

Can we say anything similar about schadenfreude's first cousin, malice? Roughly speaking, the difference between schadenfreude and malice is that schadenfreude comes into play only when another person actually has (or at least is believed to have) suffered some misfortune, while malice is subject to no such restrictions. We can maliciously want another to suffer a misfortune, maliciously fantasize about

[7] Friedrich Nietzsche, *Human, All Too Human: A Book for Free Spirits,* trans. R. J. Hollingdale (Cambridge: Cambridge University Press, 1996), p. 314.

[8] Lucretius, *On the Nature of Things,* trans. John Selby Watson (New York: Cosimo Classics, 2009), p. 54. I owe my appreciation of this and the preceding passage to Julia Driver, who cited them both in a talk that I attended a few years ago.

[9] For an account that takes schadenfreude to contribute to well-being in a somewhat different way, see Earl Spurgin, "An Emotional-Freedom Defense of Schadenfreude," *Ethical Theory and Moral Practice* 18 (2015), pp. 767–84.

inflicting it, and maliciously take pleasure in imagining its effects, even when we know that none of this will ever happen. Because malicious thoughts do not correspond to reality, they can neither release us from envy nor confirm our own relative good fortune. Nevertheless, precisely *because* they don't correspond to reality, they are well suited to provide consolations of other sorts.

Preeminent among these is a chance to take back a measure of control when we are oppressed and can do nothing about it. So, for example, after describing his craven attempts to curry favor with the teachers at his boarding school, George Orwell concludes by observing, "[A]ll the while, at the middle of one's heart, there seemed to stand an incorruptible inner self who knew that whatever one did— whether one laughed or sniveled or went into frenzies of gratitude for small favours—one's only true feeling was hatred."[10] And Jim Dixon, the protagonist of Kingsley Amis's brilliant comic novel *Lucky Jim*, has the following thoughts about his insufferable rival Bertrand Welch:

> He wished there were some issue on which he could defeat Bertrand, even at the risk of alienating his father. Any measure short of, or not necessitating too much, violence would be justified. But there seemed to be no field of endeavour where he could employ a measure of that sort. For a moment he felt like devoting the next ten years to working his way to a position as art critic on purpose to review Bertrand's work unfavourably. He thought of a sentence in a book he'd once read: "And with that he picked up the bloody old towser by the scruff of the neck, and, by Jesus, he near throttled him." This too made him smile.[11]

In cases like these, there is something deeply reassuring about giving oneself over to one's hostile feelings. It's disturbing to fear that another has taken away one's agency, and frankly acknowledging one's hatred is a way of restoring it.

[10] George Orwell, "Such, Such Were the Joys," in *A Collection of Essays by George Orwell* (Garden City, NY: Doubleday Anchor, 1956), p. 33.
[11] Kingsley Amis, *Lucky Jim* (New York: Viking Press, 1958), pp. 51–52.

Because each of these examples draws attention to a way in which forbidden thoughts can make our internal lives less painful or more pleasant, their collective tendency is to give my claim that freedom of mind enhances the quality of our experience a vaguely therapeutic cast. I think, in fact, that this aspect of mental freedom is indeed important: because even the sunniest among us are often bruised, humiliated, disappointed, and frustrated, I suspect there are few who *don't* sometimes need to think dark thoughts to bleed away their bad feelings. However, I don't want to rest too much on this, for the far more important fact about the beliefs, attitudes, and fantasies that moralists deplore is their centrality to human life and culture as we know them.

It is hard to overstate the connection between civil society and uncivil thoughts. Given the marbling of hostility, envy, resentment, and bias that runs through even (especially?) the twinkiest of sensibilities, there is an obvious need for arrangements that will prevent our antisocial thoughts from corrupting our social interactions. That need gives rise to many of the prized conventions of civilized intercourse. As Thomas Nagel puts it:

> The point of polite formulae and broad abstentions from expression is to leave a great range of potentially disruptive material unacknowledged and therefore out of play. It is material that everyone who has been around knows is there—feelings of hostility, contempt, derision, envy, vanity, boredom, fear, sexual desire, or aversion, plus a great deal of simple self-absorption.
>
> Part of growing up is developing an external self that fits smoothly into the world with others that have been similarly designed.[12]

To Nagel's observation that conventions of concealment "make civilized life possible,"[13] I would add that the kind of civilized life that they make possible is one that offers opportunities for sophisticated discrimination, delicate judgment, and highly evolved exercises of tact, and that each of these activities is a precondition for a range of

[12] Thomas Nagel, *Concealment and Exposure* (Oxford: Oxford University Press, 2002), p. 6.
[13] Ibid.

social pleasures that wouldn't even be conceivable if the conventions didn't exist.

Quite apart from this, moreover, it's just the dark corners in our minds that make each of us so endlessly interesting both to ourselves and to others. We love dogs, but we don't find their thoughts intriguing because we pretty much know (or at least think we know) what's going on in there. But each person's consciousness is a cognitive/emotional jumble, a tangled constellation of beliefs, yearning, resentments, and urges that provides an endless field for interpretation and attempts at understanding. These are precisely the challenges that elevate our interactions with others above the bare cooperative pursuit of common goals and that explain why life in society is so endlessly engaging. Who hasn't spent hours trying to work out what's really behind someone's perplexing behavior? Who hasn't wondered what an enigmatic acquaintance really cares about or what a friend's attitude toward him really is? Who can read Dostoevsky or Henry James without being struck by the complexity with which the judicious and orderly elements of our minds interact with those that are wayward and wanton and ugly? And how much of interest would be left if we all managed to *suppress* all of our wayward and wanton and ugly thoughts?

VI

With these questions, we reach the heart of my opposition to moralism. My deepest complaint is that by enjoining us to suppress our ugly fantasies, malign attitudes, and baseless prejudices, the moralists are asking us to rid ourselves of an essential part of what makes us human. I've often wondered about the appeal of a heaven that contains no tension, intrigues, or strife—just what do the numberless souls who inhabit that Kingdom *do* all day?—and I get a similar feeling about a comparable society on earth. Wouldn't it be boring to be around people who were known to think only good thoughts, and wouldn't it be stifling to have to stifle all of our own bad ones?[14] Would we even

---

[14] For discussion that answers these questions in the affirmative, see Susan Wolf, "Moral Saints," *Journal of Philosophy* 79, no. 8 (August 1982), pp. 419–39. For an

remain ourselves if we somehow managed to prune away the less sa-vory elements of what Nagel aptly describes as "the sheer chaotic, trop-ical luxuriance of the inner life"?[15]

As I see things, these questions answer themselves. We would not be selves at all if we were not able to form our own judgments and have our own feelings, and there is never a guarantee that the thoughts and feelings at which we arrive will satisfy whatever requirements morality might impose. This doesn't mean that the moralist is incapable of ed-iting his transgressive thoughts and feelings without sacrificing his selfhood, but it does raise questions both about how thoroughly he can dissociate himself from what is expunged and about his own relation to his newly G-rated consciousness. We can put up with restrictions on action precisely because they don't reach to our core—because they allow an honorable retreat to a posture of inner resistance. But no comparable retreat is possible when we internalize restrictions on our beliefs and attitudes themselves. By allowing morality to regulate our very thoughts, and thus throwing open the innermost bastion of the self, we would preside over the elimination of precisely those aspects of our consciousness from which any opposition might flow. This seems bound to impoverish our lives in at least four important ways.

First and most obviously, anyone who manages to suppress his malicious thoughts and hostile feelings will thereby flatten out his own subjectivity. His morally regulated inner life will lack many of the transgressive elements against which most of us struggle, and so he will have little firsthand acquaintance with the very impulses that morality exists to regulate. Because his tendencies to think forbidden thoughts will not be allowed to penetrate his subjectivity, his internal life will lack the sorts of emotional complexity that invite both literary treatment and the forms of self-interpretation that are its internal analogues. Overall, the moralist's success at suppressing his impermis-sible thoughts will make him far less interesting both to the world and to himself.

opposing view, see Robert Merrihew Adams, "Saints," *Journal of Philosophy* 81, no. 7 (July 1984), pp. 392–401.

[15] Nagel, *Concealment and Exposure*, p. 5.

Second, because his subjectivity will not contain these darker elements, he will lack opportunities to reflect on their sources and to come to grips with them. The task of understanding oneself is the work of a lifetime, and experience is its starting point. If the features that incline us to malice, contempt, and bias weren't down there somewhere, there would be nothing for a morality of thought to regulate. The moralist who simply throws a blanket over his resentments, hostilities, and prejudices is in a poor position either to understand what is really moving him or to try to do something about it.

Third—and crassly—a moralist of this stripe will deprive himself of certain important forms of gratification. As William Hazlitt observed, "there is a secret affinity with, a *hankering* after, evil in the human mind, and . . . it takes a perverse, but a fortunate delight in mischief, since it is a never-failing source of satisfaction."[16] This "affinity with evil" is not something to be proud of—Hazlitt's own attitude was as much deploring as gleeful—but no honest person can deny either the reality or the intensity of what he called "the pleasures of hating." Also, quite apart from this, even the most vicious of fantasies can provide us with the gratification of gaining in imagination something of which we are deprived in the actual world.

Finally, to set moral limits to what we may believe, feel, and imagine is to relinquish our mastery of the one thing that is totally and entirely ours: the vast world of subjectivity in which we can go anywhere and do anything. In that world, there are no crowds or scarcity, no feelings to be hurt or expectations to be accommodated, and no dangers to be avoided. Commanding this territory doesn't require visiting every square inch of it—as I have repeatedly stressed, it's far better if we *don't* fantasize about torturing people or raping infants—but it does require the freedom to go anywhere that our thoughts take us. One high-minded reason to treasure a freedom this complete is that it alone affords access to every factor that might have a bearing on the scope or content of morality; without such access, no full-conceived morality is possible. A less lofty reason, which I must confess means more to me, is the simple luxury of having so expansive a playground.

[16] William Hazlitt, "On the Pleasures of Hating," in Phillip Lopate, ed., *The Art of the Personal Essay* (New York: Anchor Books, 1995), pp. 189–98.

However, either way, to take morality itself to restrict our movements within this vast terrain would simply be to surrender much of our treasured freedom—a surrender that is completely unnecessary because no proponent of any major theoretical approach to morality has provided us with any good reason to take it to govern what goes on in the subjective realm.

In the end, our thoughts are gloriously and completely our own, and our beliefs, attitudes, and feelings are as exempt from moral as from political regulation. In the wild west of our minds, we are the only law, and our sovereignty is so complete that it trumps even the legislative authority of practical reason. Some of what morality calls for may still be allowed in, but only if and as far as we let it. In that most private of realms, we can do anything we want, and the only price we pay is being the kinds of people we are.

Index

For the benefit of digital users, indexed terms that span two pages (e.g., 52–53) may, on occasion, appear on only one of those pages.